NAVIGATING THE LEGAL WATERS IN THE EDUCTION ARENA

"New Educators' "Guide to Avoid the Court Room"
"Could it happen to you?"

By: Dr. Gene Wright, Ph. D.
    Dr. David Gover, Ed. D.
    Jeannie Wright and Misha Gover

PUBLISHED IN THE UNITED STATES
BY OLD SEVENTY CREEK PRESS
RUDY THOMAS, PUBLISHER
P. O. BOX 204
ALBANY, KENTUCKY 42602

ISBN-13:978-0692681039 (Old Seventy Creek Press)
EAN-10:0692681035

NAVIGATING THE LEGAL WATERS IN THE EDUCATION ARENA ©

"New Educators' Guide to Avoid
the Court Room"

"Could it happen to you?"

Dr. Gene Wright, Ph.D. and Dr. David
Gover, Ed.D.

Jeannie Wright and Misha Gover

Rudy Thomas, Managing Editor

July 10, 2016

FORWARD

Over the years there have been law books written that include wide-ranging information on many legal areas that affect teachers and administrators. In fact, most of those books are written with extensive information that pertains to what school leaders need to know to make "safe" decisions.

However, this "Law Guide" is an easy read and covers only the areas that are pertinent to the" everyday life" of school leaders. It does not encompass everything leaders need to know; nevertheless, what is included, hopefully, will keep them out of trouble and out of court.

Be it understood however, the writers of this "Law Guide" are not lawyers and make no legal recommendations regarding how to handle any legal issue.

About the Authors & Contributors ©

Gene Wright has worked as a full-time Visiting Professor for Eastern Kentucky University, teaching in the Education Leadership Program; Ethics and Counseling and Educational Psychology Departments. He has been an Adjunct Professor at the University of the Cumberlands and Union College. He is a former public school teacher, counselor, principal and Director of Pupil Personnel Services. Dr. Wright has worked at the State Department of Education as the School Improvement Director to assist district schools in closing the achievement gap. Dr. Wright earned his doctorate at Columbia Pacific University in Education Administration with emphasis on Improving Leadership Effectiveness for Public School Administrators, and Dropout Prevention Strategies.

David B. Gover has served in the public schools as a teacher, principal and superintendent. He served as Graduate Chair and Director of Leadership at the University of the Cumberlands. Currently he is Chair of Faculty Development at UC with the Rank of Professor. He has been an Associate Professor in the Educational Leadership Department at Union College, Barbourville, Kentucky and served as a consultant to several colleges, universities and public schools. Dr. Gover has been an adjunct Professor for Eastern Kentucky University in the Educational Leadership

Department and has an earned Doctorate from Indiana University in Educational Administration.

Jeanne Wright provided patient care in a variety of settings through collaboration with community and health care providers in the Central and Appalachia parts of Kentucky. Some of the *Research and Quality Improvement* methods were focused on certain communicable illnesses and health care issues relating to school-aged children and their families.

Misha W. Gover is currently a Writing Coach in the School of Education at the University of the Cumberlands with the Rank of Professor. She has worked extensively in developing the Redesigned Principalship Program and has conducted Capstone Presentations throughout Kentucky. She was Director of the Alternative Certification Program at Union College. Mrs. Gover served in the public schools of Kentucky as a Speech and Language Pathologist (CCC) and Director of Early Childhood Education.

Rudy Thomas is a poet, novelist, publisher and editor. He is the Upward Bound Director at Lindsey Wilson College in Columbia, Kentucky. Over the years Mr. Thomas served as classroom teacher in the public schools, principal and superintendent. He possesses the skills to shape, build and monitor policies and practices that promote a safe learning environment for students. Mr. Thomas is truly a "visionary" in the field of education.

Table of Contents

Navigating the Legal Waters ©

"An Educator's Guide to Avoid the Demise of Their Professional Career"

Introduction – UNDERSTANDING THE IDIOLOGY OF LAW

Schools are supposed to be a sanctuary for students to learn and teachers to teach. However, the school environment puts teachers at risk every day and could be a very perilous place for the future of their career.

This handbook is about establishing a mindset for educators to understand and to prevent the pitfalls that lurk around every corner which are capable of destroying their family, livelihood, and reputation.

All organizations have written policies which set forth guidelines to follow in the work place for performance expectations as well as setting the parameters for appropriate conduct. This applies to educators, healthcare workers, the legal professions and other types of employment that deal with the public.

 As a result of various court cases, educators are expected to comply with and enforce the policies of the organization and maintain a safe and orderly teaching and learning environment.

1

Teachers and school administrators, assuming the role of parents, *in loco parentis*, can also use reasonable actions and force, if necessary, to enforce policies which are to be in the best interest and safety of students.

In the Merriam-Webster Dictionary it states "In Loco Parentis is where school officials are acting in the place of parents". In the 21st Century, schools are more complicated and dangerous places, especially where school officials are "acting in the places of parents". The values of parents have changed. This is a litigious society where teachers and administrators must be aware of their situation and actions at all times.

It is important for school officials to be cognizant of the fact that even though when "acting in the place of parents", school administrators and teachers must understand that this does not create immunity when making decisions that affect the student's rights. The school administrator and teacher must be careful not to commit a wrongful act or invade a student's constitutional rights. (Wright and Gover)

Although this concept gives educators many of the privileges of a parent, teachers and administrators need to understand that these responsibilities of protecting the students are not without liability, particularly, if the educators' conduct falls below the acceptable standard of care expected for the specific circumstances in their role of supervision.

Each year hundreds of public and private school educators lose their jobs due to mindless lapses in judgment and not following policies. Careers are often destroyed and relationships terminated with families and friends.

In elementary and secondary schools across this country, administrators and teachers have violated the trust of parents by harassing, molesting and sexually assaulting students in their charge. Over a five-year period from 2001 to 2005 in the United States, sexual inappropriateness charges against 2,570 educators resulted in having their licenses terminated, denied and surrendered.[1]

Kentucky State Department of Education Officials reported nearly one hundred (100) instances of teacher sexual misconduct during the same period, which averages about two (2) violations a month during the school term. Nationwide, these numbers represent only a drop in the bucket of what is happening in schools across the nation. No one knows the exact number of educators who were not reported as having inappropriate conduct with students.

These numbers which have been reported may seem small compared to similar crimes committed by adults outside the teaching profession; however, the data does illustrate the necessity for teachers and administrators to become aware of what can and will happen if sound preventive measures are not taken in identifying the potential risks, when policies are not followed and incorrect decisions are made involving students. [2]

Most new teachers enter the classroom with a modest awareness of school law. Unfortunately, many new teachers entering the profession are given a brief orientation which might include: (a) an introduction to central office personnel; (b) being given a copy of the student code of conduct; (c) reviewing teacher benefits; and (d) given their room assignment and student roster. The legal aspects of being a classroom teacher are seldom mentioned.

New teachers and administrators do not have the time to commit to memory their states' annotated statutes, school board policies and regulations. This handbook has been developed as a quick study guide to help educators understand the consequences of their behavior in the course of their school responsibilities and in their private life.

This handbook provides the reader some of the basic concepts of school law that affect educators in the school environment and school related activities. It is intended to give a brief overview of some of the legal issues important for educators to know and consider while working in the school setting. This resource also provides suggested guidelines for the avoidance of litigation, and hopefully, will aid administrators and staff in applying concepts and principles of law to real-life and school-based situations.

This handbook is a guide and is not meant to serve as a legal document, but merely to enable teachers and administrators to make safe and informed decisions within the scope of supervising their students and honoring their contract with the local board of education. Within each chapter are actual court cases of teachers and administrators who "crossed the line" with their students, who were insubordinate to school/board policies, who were charged with malpractice, malfeasance, neglect of duty, and/or character unbecoming of a teacher.

It is recommended that school administrators utilize this handbook in their orientation sessions for new teachers.

Understanding the Ideology of School Law

One might ask, "Why is it necessary for new teachers to understand the principles of anticipatory or preventive law?" Some of the following answers might enable the school leader to draw their own conclusions:

- It will show teachers why it is important to make appropriate choices as a practicing educator.

- It will help teachers to understand their rights under Due Process.

- It increases the teachers' ability to protect self and students and reduce the risk of destroying their career.

- It will reduce the teachers' risk of liability situations.

- It will emphasize the importance of the teacher being an exemplar both professionally and personally, to be more effective with students, parents, and the community.

- It will enable teachers to be more cognizant of their school board policies and local school policies.

- It will give teachers the fundamental relationship between law and current issues in education.

- *IT WILL HELP TO KEEP THEM IN THE CLASSROOM AND OUT OF COURT.*

Endnotes:

1. Cincinnati Post, 2007
2. Dunklee & Shoop. *The Principal's Guide to School Law. (2006)*

Chapter One – PREPARING YOUR LEADERSHIP TEAM

Coming out of the classroom into an administrative position, teachers may have been exposed to leaders who were *managers of routine agendas or scripts* and were sometimes over *reactive* in decisions made to deal with issues. This type of leadership can be very problematic. It is important that principals understand their role and how to utilize the leadership team, i.e. teachers, assistant principals, department heads, etc., to share in the decision-making role.

Teachers preparing for a leadership role in the schools must prepare themselves with the knowledge, skills, dispositions and methods to face the fast and changing culture in the schools.

Administrators are more than disciplinarians and building supervisors. Therefore, it is important that every administrator and department head understand their role and responsibilities in the chain of command. It is the principal's responsibility to have a list of these responsibilities and a "pecking" order for the leadership team.

Many teachers, at some point in this profession, will be accepting an administrative position and hopefully, this will not be the end of their learning. Leaders need to constantly be involved in learning activities to present a model for the staff and students. It is important for educators to keep pace with technology because education is driving technology. This is apparent when educators see all the technological advances in the schools.

Attitude

Think about this: "Your attitude, not your aptitude will determine your altitude" [1] as well as your disposition and you're thinking process. Great leaders maintain a positive attitude and think about opportunities for tomorrow. Great leaders don't blame others when something goes wrong, rather they focus on the solution. Outstanding leaders see themselves as conquers over circumstances rather than victims of circumstances,

It is important to realize that leaders are optimistic. Leaders can learn valuable lessons in every problem or setback. Leaders see failures as an opportunity to make more effective decisions. An optimistic leader can be an energizer for teachers, students and staff as well as stakeholders outside the school.

Charisma

Webster's Dictionary defines "charisma" *as an extraordinary power in a person, group, cause, etc., that takes hold of popular imagination, wins popular support, etc.* [2]

Read this definition again and review various leadership styles. Charisma is a powerful word and can make or break a leader. When attitude and charisma are found in a person, those are two valuable assets for a school leader; however, it takes consistency and discipline. Being overly charismatic can also be a liability. It is important to listen twice as much as one speaks. Seven Covey's "Fifth Habit" says "seek first to understand, then be understood." [3] In other words, listen to the staff, students and parents. For example, some people only want to talk about themselves. That is not an effective trait for a leader.

Dealing with Irate Parents

If not handled effectively, dealing with parents can go badly very quickly. An effective leader will be an active listener, take copious notes, maintain eye contact and ask clarifying questions. The administrator must show a sincere interest in the parent's concern. If a student is included in the conference and doesn't show respect toward the parent, the principal must then take charge and point out the student's misbehavior/disrespect toward the parent. At this point, the administrator should summarize the parent's concern, explain the need to investigate, and set a time to contact the parents to report the findings. Also, the administrator should explain what the possible responses will be:

(1) If the parent's concern is verified, an apology is in order and a corrective action will be administered to the staff.

(2) If a different story is revealed, with verification from several observers, the discipline will stand – (could be a suspension, no participation in activities, etc.).

After concluding the conference, the administrator should walk with the parent when the parent exits the building. This will provide the opportunity to reduce anger and build more trust.

KEY POINT: Support staff members in situations, when those staff members are right, but in other instances when a staff member makes a mistake it may be necessary to take corrective action. NEVER DISCUSS THE CORRECTIVE ACTION WITH OTHERS. Always remember that in many instances angry people, (parents) just want to have someone in authority to listen to them. Listening will often diffuse a person's anger.

Firing an Incompetent Staff Member
At the school level, the only person to direct the due process procedure is the person's

immediate supervisor. For example, if a classroom teacher is shown to be incompetent, the building principal begins the process. The superintendent's responsibility is to observe the process and provide advice. Permission to contact the district's attorney should be requested when necessary.

When permission is granted, the attorney will begin the process and the superintendent will be responsible for the charges. Getting the attorney involved prior to the process and *keeping* the attorney informed throughout the procedure will insure that each step is properly executed. Steven Covey stated in his *Seven Habits of Highly Effective People* that leaders "must keep the end in mind". [4] When dismissing a teacher, the end could be facing a judge in the courtroom. Therefore, it is not fair for the school attorney to be expected to defend the dismissal process without being involved from the beginning.

The key to removing incompetent personnel is by having detailed documentation showing steps for improvement during the evaluation process. The school administrator must have everything documented, documented, documented. A statement of concerns is shown to the teacher and the teacher is encouraged to participate in developing a plan for improvement. A statement of concerns accompanied by a written improvement plan is provided for the teacher, who then, is ask to sign a statement that perhaps mirrors the following:

"I may not necessarily agree with what is stated in this conference, however, I do agree that the conference was held and that I was given a copy of the conference report".

It is important to have a witness nearby who can verify that the teacher was provided a copy of the report in case the teacher refuses to sign the statement. The witness can also verify that the signature is that of the teacher.

The district should make every effort to assist the teacher in the improvement process, and if the case ends up in court, it will, hopefully, be decided in favor of the district.

Poor classroom management is a common issue with new teachers. This is where close and frequent observations are necessary early in the semester with the novice teacher. The administrator should set a regular schedule to observe teachers and follow up with those who are questionable. After identifying the weakness of the identified staff member, a plan of action must be put in place with the goal to improve the effectiveness of that staff member.

Endnotes

1. Zig Ziegler
2. Webster Dictionary
3. Steven Covey, <u>The 7 Habits of Highly Effective People, 1989.</u>
4. <u>Ibid.</u>

Chapter Two – THE UNITED STATES CONSTITUTION AND PUBLIC EDUCATION

The Federal Constitution is recognized as the supreme law which gives each State the authority to control their educational system. It also requires the states to exercise their authority within the provisions required by the Constitution. The decision of the Supreme Court in Cooper v. Aaron made it clear that:

"It is, of course, quite true that the responsibility for public education is primarily the concern of the states, but it is equally true that such responsibilities, like all other state activity, must be exercised consistently with federal constitutional requirements as they apply to state action." [1]

Educators, especially new teachers and administrators, should develop their educational program, referencing the Bill of Rights, particularly the first Ten Amendments to the Constitution. These Amendments state the liberties that are safeguarded, but which most citizens take for granted. For example, take a brief look at the First, Fourth, Fifth, and Fourteenth Amendments in order to visualize their relationship to the educational setting.

First Amendment – *"Congress shall make no*

law respecting an establishment of religion, or prohibiting the free exercise thereof; or abridging the freedom of speech, or of the press; or the right of the people peaceably to assemble, and to petition the government for a redress of grievances."

Fourth Amendment – *Guarantees the right of people "to be secure in their persons, houses, and effects against unreasonable searches and seizures;" and "to safeguard the privacy and security of individuals, against arbitrary invasions by governmental officials."* (2)

Fifth Amendment-Stipulates that no one shall be *"compelled in any criminal case to be a witness against himself, nor be deprived of life, liberty, or property without due process of the law; nor shall private property be taken for public use, without just compensation."*

Fourteenth Amendment - The due process clause of this amendment has been influential in initiating school litigation. This amendment provides that no state shall "deny to any person within its jurisdiction, the equal protection of the laws." Teacher tenure is also protected under this amendment.

As previously mentioned, states must work within the provisions of the federal constitution, and educators must operate consistently within the parameters of state regulations and school/district polices. Although many new teachers have not been exposed to school law, teachers are not protected by being "ignorant of the laws." [3] Therefore, it is paramount, as educators read thoroughly the contents of this text, that copious notes be taken and daily reflections be competed on in-class/school experiences in order to minimize any legal pitfalls which might be encountered.

The "Bill of Rights" is the fundamental chunk of the U.S. Constitution that guarantees each person certain basic rights. What does the bill of rights consist of in the constitution? The bill of rights consists of the first ten amendments. It takes 38 states or three fourth of fifty states to ratify an amendment to the constitution. (Wikipedia, the free encyclopedia). [4] There are 27 amendments to the constitution. Those amendments have been ratified by the required number of states and are part of the Constitution.

The first ten amendments were adopted and ratified simultaneously and are known collectively as the Bill of Rights. *Robert J. Safransky.* [5]

Three of those amendments directly affect school administrators, teachers, students and other school personnel. Those amendments are listed as follows:

- The First Amendment concerns freedom of speech. The Fifth and Fourteenth Amendments protect the right to Due Process.

Look at what each of these amendments conveys in regard to the operation of a classroom as well as the actions of the school administrators, beginning with the first amendment - Freedom of Speech. There have been several court cases involving students as well as teachers that are directly affected by the First Amendment.

The most famous case involving student speech is Tinker v. Des Moines Independent Community School District (1969). [6] This is where the Supreme Court ruled that students could wear armbands protesting the Vietnam War providing there was no disruption of school activities. A high school principal at the time period the Tinker decision was adjudicated, had activist students and was dealing with issues to insure that there were not disruptions. This was a "challenge at the best". Even so, while students are afforded First Amendment freedom, their rights may be restricted.

The courts have rules that certain types of speech, including certain types of clothing and religious symbols, such as T-shirts with suggestive language or a necklace with the symbol of a cross and/or participation in

18

groups/associations must be applied in a manner that attempts to balance student's free speech rights, and the school's responsibility to provide a safe and orderly environment.

The Court noted that students can be disciplined for lewd speech in Bethel School District No. 403 v. Fraser (1986). [7] Then in Morse v. Fredrick (2007) [8] the Court reasoned that school officials could prevent a student from displaying a message that appeared to endorse drug use as the student watched the Olympic torch pass the front of the school. Considering the rights of teachers, the Supreme Court recognized that teachers could address matters of public concern in Pickering v. Board of Education of Township High School District 205, Will County (1968) [9] as described below.

"Pickering involved a Township High School teacher who was dismissed after writing a letter to a local newspaper which criticized how the Township Board of Education and the district superintendent had handled past proposals to raise new revenue for the schools. The claim that his writing the letter was protected by the First and Fourteenth Amendments was rejected by the Board of Education. He appealed the Board's action to the Circuit Court of Will County and then to the Supreme Court of Illinois, which both affirmed his dismissal. The Supreme Court of the United States agreed the

teacher's First Amendment right to free speech were violated and reversed the decision of the Illinois Supreme Court." (Wikipedia, the Free Encyclopedia). [10]

The Fifth and Fourteenth Amendments specifically address "due process". The Fifth Amendment grants specific rights to persons accused of crimes and it requires the federal government to follow specific procedures in dealing with citizens. When school officials question students about misbehavior in schools, the students are not entitled to the warning that the Supreme Court established in Miranda v. Arizona (1966). [11] This is known in law enforcement to "Mirandize" someone by reading the following: "You have the right to remain silent, the right to legal counsel, and that anything he/she says can be used in court against him/her."

The due process clause guarantees basic fairness. In Gross v. Lopez, [12] the Court considers what due process means for students facing temporary suspension from school because of their alleged violations of school discipline rules. The Court concluded that the accused students must be afforded an informal hearing with school administrators before each suspension. In Ingraham v. Wright, [13] the issue was whether a hearing of some sort must precede corporal punishment by a school teacher. Finally, Horwitz v. Board of Curators considered the procedures required before a student may be dismissed for academic failure. *(Board of Curators of the University of Missouri ET AL. v. Horowitz Supreme Court of the United States 435 U.S> 7, March 1, 1978)* [(14)]

Where did the principal go wrong?
What is his liability?
WHAT! -- Schooler to Confess to being a Terrorist

"EAST ISLIP, NY (CNN) - The mother of a middle school student in New York says the school's principal tried to get her son to confess his allegiance to ISIS. Her son, Nashawn Uppal, admits he said something he shouldn't have, but he said he was only defending himself against a bully. His mother said he was told to write a false confession saying he was a terrorist and now she wants two school administrators fired. He said he was called a terrorist repeatedly and asked what he would blow up next. Nashawn said he was pulled out of class right before the school day ended. He was brought in to a room with the school's principal, Mark Bernard and assistant principal, Jason Stanton. "He started yelling at me to write you are a part ISIS and you would blow up the school," Uppal said. Nashawn says he was told by both Bernard and Stanton to write down he was a member of ISIS, a terrorist and would blow up the school. The 12-year-old said he would not. Nashawn's mother, Nubaisha Amar, said she was waiting for her son at dismissal while he was allegedly being

21

interrogated. She said she never received a call from the school about her son's whereabouts until two hours later. Local police were called, and her son was questioned by officers, and the family even consented to having their home searched. Police said they found nothing at the home and found no signs of wrongdoing by Uppal. They said this was a case of boys being boys, and yet, Uppal was suspended by the district for five days. "Nothing makes sense and it was like I didn't have a second of a chance to talk to my son alone, what happened? This principal is supposed to call me," Uppal's mother said. Amar believes administrators not only harassed her son, but also fabricated their version of events. Superintendent John Dolan denied the allegations and in a statement said a fair and appropriate disciplinary process is underway and the district has no further comment at this time. When asked if the bully Nashawn referred to in his version of events was ever disciplined, the district also would not comment. Nashawn's mother says she is not comfortable with the idea of her son going back to East Islip Middle School". (KASA ENB News Briefing, January 14, 2016). [15]

Endnotes:

1. *Cooper v. Aaron,* 358 U.S. 1 (1958).
2. *Carmara v. Municipal Court of City and County of San Francisco*, 387 U.S., 523, 528 (1967).
3. *Wood v. Strickland*, 420 U.S. 308 (1975).
4. *Wikipedia, the Free Encyclopedia.*
5. *Robert J. Safransky.*
6. Tinker v. Des Moines Independent Community School District (1969).
7. Bethel School District No. 403 v. Fraser (1986).
8. Morse v. Fredrick (2007).
9. Pickering v. Board of Education of Township High School District 205, Will County (1968).
10. Wikipedia, the Free Encyclopedia.
11. Miranda v. Arizona (1966).
12. Gross v. Lopez, (1975).
13. Ingraham v. Wright, (1977).
14. *Board of Curators of the University of Missouri ET AL. v. Horowitz Supreme Court of the United States 435 U.S> 7, March 1, (1978)*

Additional Case References:

1. *Abbott v. Burke,* 575 A.2d 359 (N.J. 1990).
2. *Minnesota Federation of Teachers v.*

Nelson, 740 F. Supp.694, D. Minn. (1990).

3. *New Jersey v. T.L.O.*, 469 U.S. 325 (1985).
4. *Pickering v. Board of Education of Township High School District* 205, 391 U.S. 563 (1968).
5. *Rose v. Council for Better Education,* 790 S.W.2d 186 (Ky. 1989).
6. *San Antonio Independent School District v. Rodriguez,* 411 U. S. 1, 42 (1973).
7. *Tinker v. Des Moines Independent Community School district,* 393 U.S. 503 (1969).

Chapter Three – MANAGING AND ORGANIZING YOUR CLASSROOM

Training courses should have prepared each teacher extensive training in classroom management and organization skills, working with kids of different levels of ability, differential instruction, multiracial and multicultural groups, etc. Many teachers have experienced or are experiencing a rude awakening from theory to reality on how to meet the academic needs and close the achievement gap for all students.

Teachers can no longer find a comfort zone in the classroom, as they are held accountable for meeting the state and federal mandates. Professional teachers as well as administrators should not stay on the "Path of Complacency", but should investigate and implement best practices and collaborate with colleagues on the various ways to improve student performance. [1]

Teachers are experiencing an incredible amount of stress due to these demands. Teachers are expected to be "experts" and competent in all aspects of the education process especially when addressing classroom discipline and management.

Managing the Classroom

The successful management of a classroom seems simple and easy, but it is not. There are several decisions that must take place to insure that all students learn at high levels as well as the effective promotion of a safe and orderly classroom. Teachers and school administrators must make decisions that will protect their integrity and limit their liability. Here are just a few suggestions:

Decision #1:

The successful teacher must understand what the district policies require regarding the limits the teacher has in organizing the classroom. The teacher needs to know what the limits are in regard to classroom rules and procedures. (Wright and Gover)

Decision #2:

The teacher's communication with the principal is very important. It is essential, if the teacher is new to the school, to meet with the principal to discuss those limits and to determine whether the rules and regulations that the teacher plans to use are within the policies and the guidelines that can be supported by the principal. The guidance that the teacher should get from this meeting is critical to the teacher's success in the classroom, for without the support of the principal a teacher's tenure in that school will be limited. (Wright and Gover)

Decision #3:

It is important that the teacher has a clear understanding of the difference between a rule and a procedure. A rule is for the purpose of controlling student behavior that requires consequences. Procedures outlined in this process will become routine and should have positive consequences. A procedure determines how the teacher conducts the classroom and a rule describes how students will conduct themselves in the classroom. (Wright and Gover)

Decision #4:

What the teacher does prior to the student's arrival to class will have a pronounced effect on the success the first day students are present. Make sure that the classroom is highly organized. The teacher should review the folder (electronic) of each student to learn as much information as possible before meeting the students. View the student's picture, grades, test scores and discipline problems if any and be prepared to call each student by name as they enter the classroom on the first day of school. This will assure that all **students** understand that the teacher is in charge of the classroom and demands respect from all the students. (Wright and Gover)

Decision #5:

The rules and procedures should be posted in a conspicuous place in the classroom. Discussing the rules and procedures with the students is paramount as well as the consequences for breaking the rules. A copy of the rules should be available for the students to insert in their notebook. The emphasis must be on insuring that the rules and procedures are for the purpose of seeing that each student learns at high levels and the classroom is conducted in an orderly and safe manner. (Wright and Gover)

Reduce Litigation Liability

Educators should realize that it is a fact, that in today's society, the liability of being a teacher, principal, etc., can be very volatile, especially when litigation is involved. Therefore, it is paramount for educators to stay within the boundaries of the institution's rules and policies and are not at fault when there were no arbitrary or negligent decisions. It is significantly critical that all administrators and teachers understand that teachers are responsible for their actions. In some cases, improper actions could result in the loss of licenses and could result in charges that could end the teacher's career. It could even include incarceration. (Wright and Gover)

Here are several actions that principals and teachers should put in place to lessen their liability:

28

- Teachers must make every effort to insure that the classroom is a safe place. This means that the teacher takes charge of the classroom and manages the classroom in a safe and orderly manner.

- Teachers new to the school, should collaborate with seasoned teachers to learn about how a successful classroom is managed.

- Every teacher must be aware of certain situations that could be dangerous to students. Not being aware of those situations could be viewed as negligent behavior. Here are just a few examples: a) leaving the classroom unattended, b) mediocre supervision of students on the playground, c) permitting students to act out in the classroom, d) failure to discipline students that are creating a disturbing situation. There are many additional examples; however, just a few have been named here. (Wright and Gover)

- An administrator and teacher must maintain a level head and use sound judgment in every action and/or decision. It is important to consider the unanticipated consequences of one's decision. It's also important to keep calm, cool, and collected when making decisions. (Wright and Gover)

Aware of Your Liability

Professor Martha McCarthy in 1992 stated, "The first element that must be determined in a negligence case is — duty to protect. This is an integral part of a teacher's responsibilities.

Teachers and administrators have a responsibility to anticipate potential dangers and to take precautions to protect their students from those activities which include acceptable supervision of students who are engaged in high risk activities." Those high risk activities could be classified as follows: field trip away from school to a location that could be risky, transportation to and from an activity, lack of proper supervision in the classroom, lack of proper supervision in the hall way, or an activity where bullying could take place."

If a school employee fails to take reasonable steps to protect a student from injury, the employee can be found negligent. In negligence cases, courts will weigh the actions of a teacher or an administrator against how a reasonable teacher or administrator would have acted in a similar situation. Failure to exercise a reasonable standard of care must be proven in a negligence case." [2]

Incompetence

Incompetency is usually defined in broad categories such as, "lack of ability, legal qualifications, or fitness to discharge the required duty.

Tenured teachers believe they are fully protected under the tenure law, but this law is designed for schools to "assure competent teachers continued employment as long as their performance is satisfactory."[3]

In the case of, *Stamper v. Bd. Of Educ., in Illinois,* [4] a teacher with nineteen years of extraordinary service in the second grade, ask to be transferred to teach seventh and eighth grade home economics. This request was granted. After two years in the new assignment, the teacher began receiving warning and deficiency notices relating to poor classroom performance. It became apparent, after three more years, of incompetence, such as letting students leave the classroom at their convenience, not monitoring classroom assignments, not maintaining an orderly classroom environment, that teacher would have to be dismissed. The board did terminate the teacher's position. [5]

States that have initiated the "non-tenured" policy for new teachers to allow school administrators to assess whether these novice teachers possess the knowledge, disposition and skills to be effective in the classroom before qualifying for the tenure tract. Unfortunately, some incompetent teachers manage to acquire the tenured position because of the incompetency of the administrator failing to evaluate the teachers during the transition period.

Some parents can be very aggressive in accusing teachers of being negligent and lackadaisical in their instructional methods. These complaints should never happen if the school administrator actively evaluates a teacher's instructional practice and performance in the classroom. Valid complaints such as those mentioned above, not only place the teacher at risk for dismissal, but also the school administrator for neglect of duty.

Teachers have been "fired" for ineffective teaching, not having the capacity for having order in the classroom, being disorganized, having a messy classroom, and being insubordinate. One case involving teacher incompetency was upheld in the Commonwealth Court of Appeals of Pennsylvania on the grounds that the teacher's behavior and conduct in the classroom was unprofessional, and failing to maintain her composure with her colleagues and parents, which is expected of a teacher. [6]

A Pennsylvania case involved a teacher who was helping her husband in a "beer garden," where the teacher also entertained customers by serving beer, drinking with them and also playing the pin ball machine. [7] Although this is a dated case and is in the category of teacher as exemplar, it still represents a message about how teachers should conduct their personal life.

Insubordination –"Pushing the Button"

Insubordination, as defined by the courts: A "willful disregard of expressed or implied directions of the employer and a refusal to obey reasonable orders. [8]

In this case, a teacher in a Kansas school had requested to be relieved from the assigned duties during the final week of school. Obviously, the request was not approved, given the importance of having all teachers on duty during this crucial time of the instructional school year. The teacher used sick days for that week to go for a job interview. The principal of the school in Texas giving the interview called the Kansas principal for a recommendation for the teacher who had taken "sick" days. The call confirmed the teacher was being insubordinate and untruthful by falsifying the sick leave document, and obviously, this conduct was unauthorized.

Teachers can also be dismissed for violation of administrative regulations and school board policies. One must keep in perspective that there is not a relationship between classroom performance, and a teacher's conduct. [9] Insubordination is normally tied to rules and regulations, and one's noncompliance to these

33

rules is easily documented. One example is when a teacher, on several occasions, refused to complete the performance evaluation, and was dismissed on charges of being insubordinate to school board policy. [10]

Another case involved the termination of a high school counselor for failing to keep track of graduation requirements for seniors who were scheduled to graduate.

The counselor was responsible for making sure that students who needed classes to graduate would be registered for such. The counselor neglected to do so and did not know which students were having academic difficulty. Even worse, the counselor failed to contact the parents to make them aware of their child's academic deficiencies. The counselor was terminated on grounds of neglect of duty and unprofessional conduct. [11]

A Principal in Nevada violated the school district's leave policy which allowed administrators to take five school days per year or two days in succession of accumulated leave days. The principal had promised his son, who had gone to Europe on a two-year mission commitment, to meet the son in Europe at the end of the commitment and fly back to the states with him. The principal, who had accumulated 40 leave days, had planned on using ten [12] of those days to make the trip to Europe as planned. The principal submitted the request to the superintendent, and it was denied as per school district policy. The principal ignored the denial and went to Europe. After returning from the ten-day excursion, the principal was given a suspension notice which also included procedures for dismissal of duties and employment. The principal sued the district and the district's defense was that of "insubordination." The attorney for the district argued that the principal "willfully disregarded implied directions, and had such a defiant attitude to be equivalent thereto." The case was appealed to the Supreme Court of Nevada who therein *reversed* the dismissal charges on the grounds that the students were not adversely affected by the principal's absence, and the principal had made "an error of judgment resulting in no harm to his employers." (13) This case appeared to be a "no brainer" on how the courts should have ruled, and is an example of how one's reputation still can be tainted even though the court rules in the defendant's favor. The shadow of guilt will always linger in the minds of many.

Neglect of Duty

Neglect of duty occurs when a person doesn't fulfill duties expected of them as per the contract. It often occurs in the work place when the supervisor gets "buddy-buddy" with staff and the work environment gets too lax. Failing to carry out the assigned duties can result in termination. When administrators try to please all the staff and ignore crucial supervisory functions, the work ethic of the staff has a tendency to deteriorate. Regardless of the leadership style of the administrator, teachers are still responsible and liable for following school board policy and honoring their contractual agreement with the board. Some of the areas of neglect issues are: Leaving a classroom unattended [14], inappropriately supervising students while on a school related trip, [15] or not complying with local school board professional development requirements, as in the case of an Oklahoma teacher. [16]

There are many neglect cases which involved teachers not carrying out assigned responsibilities while supervising students. For example, a teacher was dismissed when persistently refusing to update the students' cumulative records for review by the accreditation team. [17] An appalling case in Louisiana resulted in a teacher being terminated when three children with special needs were locked in a closet so work could be done on unrelated tasks. [18]

Administrators, supervisors and teachers have a contractual obligation to provide an environment of protection for their employees and students. [19]

Unauthorized Sick Leave

This is an area, if seriously investigated, could result in "grief" for many educators. Although, it seems acceptable for a person to take a "mental" day or two because of experiencing a toxic environment in the workplace, rather than an inviting one, such may not be the case.

A very interesting case happened in Kentucky when a teacher signed his sick leave documents, and later ended up losing the teaching position in the school district. The teacher has used a "sick day" to drive a coal truck loaded with coal across the state line. Before unloading the coal, the weight of the truck with coal had to be taken, documents signed by the driver, etc. The documents were used as artifacts against the teacher in a hearing where the teacher was charged of falsifying his sick leave request [20].

An employee in the Philadelphia school district lost the job because of excessive tardiness to the work place. The defense was that of a mental disability (personality disorder) which the employee was unable to control. The court ruled in favor of the school district on grounds that the district did not have the responsibility to compensate for a personality disorder. [21]

A teacher in Connecticut was dismissed for insubordination for taking two "sick" days to be with the spouse on a business trip. The

Supreme Court of Connecticut ruled in the teacher's favor and not for dismissal, but recommended a reprimand of a five (5) day suspension. [22]

A teacher in Maine was told not to take a week's leave of absence to visit friends in Jamaica. The suggestion from the administration was ignored and the teacher did not report for teaching duties for a week. The trip was viewed as unproductive for the school district and therefore resulting in the Superintendent recommending the teacher's dismissal for failure to honor the contract. The teacher sued and the court ruled in favor of the school district. [23]

The use of sick leave is not to be abused and should not be abused. It is not for the purpose of "shopping, vacation time, long weekends, or driving children to out of town ballgames. Educators should always consider the consequences of their actions before making decisions which could result in termination of employment, humiliating the family and destroying a career.

A teacher in a Western Kentucky School District had been out of school on several occasions and used sick leave so that the monthly check would not be docked for the days missed. Someone in the community contacted the Board of Education Member(s) and reported that the teacher was not sick; however, there was no proof provided to substantiate that the teacher was not sick. This was just a rumor. A few days later, in a regular board meeting, the board voted not approve the teacher's request to use sick leave for the days missed. In other words, the Board denied the sick leave pay. In a normal request, sick leave would have been automatically approved unless there were valid circumstances to deny the request for sick leave. The Teachers Association then provided legal counsel for the teacher and sued the Board to reinstate the teacher's request to use sick leave as originally requested in the signed sick leave statement. The court held for the teacher and the board had to pay court cost as well as the sick leave that the teacher had requested. (Wright and Gover)

Endnotes:

1. Get off the Calf Path. "Activating those Pupil Personnel Services to help Close the Achievement Gap. Wright, G., Gover, D., Loudenback, E. Cardinal Publishing's, Lexington, Ky. 2008. Professor Martha McCarthy in (1992).
2. McCarthy, (1992).
3. McCarthy, (1992).
4. Henry Black, black's Law Dictionary, 6th ed. (St. Paul, MN: West publishing Co., 1990), p 765
5. *Stamper v. Bd. Of Edu., 491 N.E.2d 36 (Ill. App.1st Dist. 1986)*
6. *Board of Edu. of school district, district of Philadelphia v. Kechner*, 109 Pa. commonwealth 120, 530 A.2d 541 (Pa. 1987)
7. *Hamburg v. North Penn School District,* 484 A.2d 867 (Pennsylvania Commonwealth, 1984).
8. *Horosko v. school dist. Of township of Mt. Pleasant*, 6 A.2d 866 (Pa. 1939), *cert.denied,* 308 US. 553 (1939).
9. Essex, Nathan L. "A Teacher's Pocket Guide to School Law. Pearson Education, Inc. Allyn and Bacon, Boston, Mass., 2006.
10. *School district No. 8, Pinal County v. Superior Court*, 102 Ariz 478, 433 P.2d 218 (1967)
11. *Gaylord v. Bd of Educ., School district.* 218, 794 p.2d. 307 (Kansas APP.1990)
12. *Sutherby v. Gobles Board of Education*, 348 N.S. 2d. 277 (Mich. Ct. App. 1984).
13. *Rust v. Clark County School District*, 683 P.2d 23 (Nev. 1984)
14. *Bickford v. Board of Education*, 336 N.W.2d 73 (Neb. 1983)

15. *Ray v. Minneapolis Bd. Of Education, Special School District No. 1*, 202 N.W. 2d 375, 378 (Minn. 1972).
16. *Harrah Independent School District v. Martin*, 440 U.S. 194. (1979).
17. *Gaulden v. Lincoln Parish School* Board, 554 So. 2d 152 (Louisiana Ct. 1989).
18. *Cunningham V. Franklin Parish School Bd.*, 554 So.2d 152 (La. Ct.APP. 1989).
19. *McCarthy, M.M. & Cambron-McCabe, N.H.* (1992) Public School Law: Teachers' and Student's Rights (3rd Ed.). Boston: Allyn & Bacon.
20. *Blaine v. Moffat County School Dist. RE No. 1*, 748 P.2d 1280 (Colo. 1988).
21. *Philadelphia School District v. Friedman*, 507 A.2d 882 (Pennsylvania Commonwealth, 1986).
22. *Tucker v. Board of Education,* 418 A.2d 933 (Conn. 1979).
23. *Fernald v. City of Ellsworth Superintending School* Comm., 342 A.2d 74 (Me. 1975).

Additional Court Cases

1. *Beilan v. Board of Public Education of Philadelphia,* 357 U.S. 399 (1958).
2. *Mims v. West Baton Rouge Parish School Board*, 315 So.2d 349 (La.Ct.App. 1975).
3. *Saunders v. Anderson,* 746 S.W.12d 185. (Tenn. 1987).
4. *Aulwurm v. Board of Education of Murphysboro Community Unit School District,* 186, 367 N.E.2d 1337 (Illinois, 1997).
5. *Mott v. Endicott School District,* No 309, 713 P.2d 98, 101. (Washington, 1986).
6. *Fernald v. City of Ellsworth Superintending School Comm., 3342 A.2d 704 (Me.1975).*

Chapter Four – DISCIPLINE AND SUPERVISION

Any organization, including schools, should operate under the concept of providing a safe and orderly environment for its employees and clients. All stakeholders must respect and follow the rules and regulations that govern the organization. The school, being a specialized organization, governed by state, school board policies and regulations, is expected to honor and implement such policies. In addition, the school must ensure that all students, staff, and other appropriate stakeholders, comply with the rules, policies, and procedures during the school day, and school functions, including overnight trips.

Many student behavior problems in the classroom originate from poor classroom management. This lack of control usually happens when the teacher gets too "cozy" with the students and neglects and/or ignores school district policies. It is the responsibility of all teachers to establish and enforce classroom rules for governing and controlling the conduct of students. These rules are to be reasonable and supplement the school board's rules and administrative regulations. This awesome responsibility must be intrinsic.

Teachers are given the authority to enforce reasonable rules not only in the classroom, but with other students in the school. For novice teachers, it is important to maintain a cool, calm, and professional posture when enforcing school rules. Acting within the perimeters of school policies entitles the teacher to safely apply the school rules.   Under common law, "in *loco parentis"*, teachers have the duty and expectations to protect students from harm and maintain classroom order. This also applies at school sponsored functions.

In the Paducah Independent School District, a kindergarten student was allowed to go to the restroom unescorted. [1] The principal received a call from the parent wanting to know why the child was sent home unescorted. The principal was unaware that the child had left the building, or was allowed to go to the rest room unescorted. The questions to be considerd are: Who is liable? Should the teacher be disciplined? Should the principal be disciplined? Do you think this breach of school policy will go to court?

Because there is a certain standard established by law for people to be protected, teachers' actions sometimes fall below that standard in protecting students against unreasonable risk. Failing to provide this duty of care when supervising students can and will result in litigation if a student is injured. In the case, *Gammon v. Edwardsville (1980), a guidance counselor failed to follow up on a complaint by*

43

an eighth grade student (girl) that was afraid of being harmed by another student who had made verbal threats. The student making the threats was called to the counselor's office and told that fighting was not allowed and would not be tolerated. A physical confrontation took place between the two students and the student who had made the complaint was injured seriously. Litigation followed and the court ruled in favor of the injured student. This was an act of nonfeasance, or failure to act appropriately. [2]

Another act of negligence is found in *Libby v. West Coast Rock Co., Inc.,* when a student on lunch break had fallen into a ditch while trying to catch a football. The student was injured and the court ruled in favor of the student. The principal of the school was aware of the hazard and failed to act in a proper manner warning the students of the danger. [3] A similar situation would apply to teachers if they are aware of a potential hazard in their classroom, such as a TV or other heavy items on shelves used as storage space and that no warning is provided for the student of the danger. The teachers should also document that appropriate supervisors have been notified.

Adequate supervision is paramount before and after school for a reasonable amount of time as students congregate to enter and exit the school. A principal failing to provide adequate information regarding rules for students to follow during these critical times of the school day could present a serious problem. When the principal fails to assign supervisory staff, this can result in litigation if a student is injured after entering school grounds. [4] This scenario can also apply to teachers if they fail to be at their assigned room when students are waiting to report to homeroom or class and a student is injured during an unsupervised confrontation with another student.

Student Code of Conduct

All states have statutes and administrative regulations which set protocol to follow for schools to create a student code of conduct to include discipline guidelines, involvement in decision-making, expression, procedural due process, etc. [5] Each student must receive a copy of this document to take home to parents/guardians. This document provides the opportunity for students and parents to know the governance of the school in relationship to expected student behavior and the consequences for violating the rules.

Corporal Punishment and Student Rights

When enforcing the school discipline code, administrators and teachers must keep in mind that the right of due process is guaranteed under the Fifth Amendment. Regardless of the violation of school rules, students must be afforded due process before relieved of any rights. [6] In other words, there has to be a balance of student rights and the responsibility of the school to ensure that discipline is maintained in a fair and equitable method. For example, the procedures set forth under the Kentucky Statute, KRS 160.295, outlines the rights of students for schools in the Commonwealth. These are:

- "Right of expression……….

- Right to participate in decision-making procedures having a direct effect on students.

- Right to receive academic grades only upon academic performance.

- Right to freedom from abuse and threat of abuse by members of school faculties and administration personnel.

- Right of access by a student to the student's own records and guarantee of the confidentiality of a student's academic records outside of the school system, except upon written authorization of the student or the student's parents or guardians." [7]

Educators in all states should become familiar with the applicable statutes and administrative regulations relating to job responsibilities. This knowledge will be added insurance of protection against potential liability in a teaching career.

Corporal punishment is legal under the Kentucky Constitution and each state is to decide on whether or not it will be permitted to be implemented in the public schools. A state permitting corporal punishment usually allows the local school board to develop a policy for the administering of corporal punishment as part of the discipline code.

From a liability point of view for teachers and administrators, corporal punishment can be high risk and these authors do not advocate the use of corporal punishment to change student behavior. It is the responsibility of school certified personnel to protect students from harm and undue punishment while under a teacher's supervision.

Every day teachers and administrators get caught up in the legal system for crossing the line and making inappropriate decisions affecting students. The use of corporal punishment is no exception. [8] It is the severity of the punishment that determines the seriousness of the liability. If an administrator or teacher administers corporal punishment, what evidence does the teacher/administrator have that the child being punished wasn't already bruised. Perhaps, the student is a victim of physical abuse at home, the parent or guardian now has an opportunity to allege that the "school" is responsible for the bruises.

In the 3rd Circuit Jurisdiction, a student alleged that an assistant principal injured the student's back when "pushing" the student. This particular student was a continuous problem for administrators, teachers and some students. The student had been suspended from school and violated the suspension by going back to school while on suspension.

The female student went directly to the classroom to have a confrontation with another female student over a boyfriend. Security was called and ordered the girl to leave the building, which the student refused to do and continued to make threats to the other student. The disruptive student was taken to the Assistant Principal's office. The female student alleged that the Assistant Principal continually yelled at this student to shut up and pushed the student on the shoulder, causing the student to back into the door jam. The student testified, "It's [sic] not like he pushed me to try to knock me over or anything. He didn't! It's [sic] not like he hauled off [and] cold-cocked me out. It wasn't like that. He was just in a fit of rage, and he was mad. And he was yelling, and it happened." The student said she had chronic back pain ever since the incident and had been treated by doctor and was not to do any type of strenuous activities. The student brought suit based on the allegation that the14[th] Amendment had been violated. The lower court favored the district and was upheld/affirmed by a higher court. [(9)]

A court of law will not relieve a teacher or administrator of liability for unreasonable actions of corporal punishment resulting in an injury or bruising.[(10)] A witness to this type of abuse, if it is not reported, as required by law, will also be liable. An example of an unreported abuse by a teacher aide resulted in dismissal from a Kentucky school district. The aide observed the teacher physically abusing a special needs child and reported the incident to the principal and the child's parent. The principal did not make a report to a law enforcement agency, but the parent reported the incident to the social service agency. The agency investigated and found that the allegation of abuse did take place. The school district dismissed the teacher aide because of being a witness to the abuse and not reporting it to an official law enforcement agency. The principal and the teacher who administered the abuse were suspended from their duties for a week with pay. Was justice served? Although this made one of the local papers as a news item, there was not a record of court proceedings.

In the state of Michigan, an alleged abuse of a severely disabled student who was nine years old, unable to walk properly, and required diapering, became extremely complicated before going to court. It all started when a teacher's aide noticed disturbing and abnormal "conditions" in the young girl's genitals. Becoming alarmed, the aide told the teacher who also witnessed the condition. This was reported to the principal who also observed the student and the teacher was instructed by the principal to notify a female state policeman of the sexual abuse team.

The State trooper didn't observe the student until four days later and also suspected sexual abuse. At that time, the trooper instructed the school personnel to contact this state trooper if additional evidence of suspected sexual abuse was noticed. Three months went by and the school called the female state trooper regarding more suspected abuse of the young girl. Keep in mind the time frame! The principal was instructed by the trooper to take the young girl to the doctor for an examination. This action was taken without the parents' notification. The trooper or school officials did not go through proper channels to get a court order for the doctor's examination, neither was any investigation completed regarding whether it was legal to go through these steps. The state trooper contacted social services to have someone meet the trooper at the doctor's office, where a social worker signed the consent form for authorization of the exam. This social worker was not the legal guardian and had not contacted the parents. The exam results came out negative for sexual abuse and the information was given to the state trooper. This information was not shared with the school officials. This did not stop the trooper from taking charge and botching the situation from bad to worse. The parents of the young girl were visited and the father was accused of sexually abusing the child. This was an attorney's dream come true.

The school officials were immune as per the law: "A person acting in good faith , makes a report, cooperates in an investigation, or assists in any other requirement of this act, is immune from civil or criminal liability." The social worker and state trooper were not immune because they exceeded their authority by authorizing the exam. If there had been evidence that the young girl's health was in serious danger or a court order obtained, both the trooper and social worker would have been protected. [11]

Child Abuse has a broad interpretation and lawyers can have a field day with corporal punishment practices in the schools. Every day teachers and administrators are caught up in the legal system for crossing the line with students because they allow emotions to control actions. Unfortunately, this can happen when using corporal punishment as a means to change behavior.

Child Abuse Law in Kentucky

Under the Child Abuse Law, "anyone who is a witness to or suspects a child is being abused, is required to report the abuse to an "official" law enforcement agency. A principal of the school is not a law enforcement agency. If one witnesses or suspects the abuse and doesn't report it to the proper authorities, this person will end up in court. (12)

WHEN TO REPORT: When there is reason to believe a child is being abused, neglected or is dependent, call the child protection hotline at 1-877-597-2331 or the county Department for Community Based Services. If in doubt, it is preferred that the person call and talk over what has come to their attention. Child Protection Services will help in sorting things out, such as whether a specific incident must be reported and to whom. If it is felt that the child is in imminent danger or is in need of immediate protection, a call to 911 or the local police department must be made. For example, a very young child or handicapped child who is left alone with no adult supervision needs immediate help. Police officers can remove a minor from a threatening environment in order to protect the child if the child is in danger of imminent death or serious physical injury or is being sexually abused and the custodian is unable/unwilling to protect the child. KRS 620.040(5)(c). [13]

Using Reasonable Judgment

Most court cases involving educators are a result of poor decision making and poor judgment. A case in point is the *Raleigh v. Independent School District (1979) law suit.* This was an era when racial tensions were extremely volatile and poor judgment was used in requiring students to attend a controversial movie, entitled *King*, which was inundated with racial slurs adding to the unrest regarding diversity issues in the school. [13]

An example of not using reasonable judgment happened when a third grade female student was sent to the principal's office for hitting a male student who had kicked the female student. A teacher was asked by the principal to hold the student upside down by the ankles while the child was paddled. The principal allegedly struck the student five times on the legs, between the knees and the waist causing welts and bruises. A few months later the same student was before the principal to receive another paddling. After a couple of licks with the paddle, the student refused to be paddled anymore. The principal summoned a male administrative assistant to force the female student to bend over a chair for more paddling. During a struggle, the student fell back against the principal's desk and injured the student's back. Finally, the student submitted to continuation of the corporal punishment which resulted in severe bruising on the buttock. The student brought suit against the principal and other school officials. The U.S. District Court ruled in favor of the school district, but an appeal to the U.S. Court of Appeals resulted in this Court overruling the U.S. District Court decision in favor of the student. [14]

School Sponsored Field Trips

Educators are responsible for providing proper supervision during school sponsored field trips. Negligent supervision, or improper supervision, seems to be the most common cause of injuries occurring to students. Teachers who have not provided adequate rules and instructions to follow during school sponsored trips leave themselves vulnerable for potential legal problems. [15]

One hundred and ten (110) students were on a field trip in Tennessee. The group stopped at a fast-food place for lunch and a short break. Several of the students ask to cross the street to a public park. The teacher agreed and one of student was hit and injured by a car while crossing the street. Litigation followed and the teacher was sued for negligence because the teacher did not escort the students across the busy street. Although the Tennessee Court of Appeals reversed the decision of the Circuit Court in finding the teacher liable of negligence, the stress and associated guilt by others that the teacher had to deal with was not pleasant. [16]

Play Ground Activities (*Recess*)

School districts have a duty to provide reasonable care to protect students against any hazardous situations on school property. This includes all playground equipment available for students to use. Adequate supervision is also expected in order to keep children from risk of harm or injury and constant monitoring is paramount. For example, if a teacher observes and allows "roughhousing" to take place while under the teacher's supervision, which results in a student injury, the teacher becomes *liable* for litigation. [17]

An interesting and very common situation happened in Indiana where an elementary student, second grader, was seriously injured when this student and another student collided head on. No, they weren't driving, but running as kids that age like to do when on the playground.

Several teachers were assigned to "monitor" the playground activities as part of their duties. This appeared to an excessive number of staff monitoring the activities of one hundred and eighty-eight elementary students. The lower court ruled in favor of the school, but the Appeals Court, based upon sufficient evidence, decided that the teachers were inattentive to the behavior of the students and should have foreseen the possibility of an accident of this sort happening [18]

It is not uncommon to observe a group of teachers during a recess break congregating in a group and appearing not to be giving adequate attention to the activities of the students. Although it is not possible to give every student personal supervision during this time of activity, it is expected that students have been given "rules of conduct" when released for recess, school sponsored trips, etc. Without adequate documentation that rules were given and even posted in the classroom, an educator's liability increases if a student accident or injury happens. Teachers should also do an immediate check for any faulty equipment or problematic areas for danger to students. Although this may not be the responsibility of teachers, it can reduce a lot of agony and stress if a student is injured while under the teacher's watch.

School Attendance and Record Keeping

All fifty states have a compulsory attendance law requiring every school age child to attend school on a regular basis. The required ages required for attendance are normally from six to sixteen, but may vary from state to state. This law originally did not include private schools as a place for students to comply with the law. It was not until 1925 that private schools were allowed to meet the requirements of the compulsory attendance laws for students enrolled in their schools. [19] In the case of *Pierce v. Society of Sisters which* challenged the Compulsory Attendance Statute of Oregon requiring students to attend public school, was overturned by the Supreme Court. [20]

It is essential to record and maintain daily attendance records. Parents expect the school personnel to be accountable for their children from the time a child enters the school bus in the morning until that child gets home after school dismisses for the day. Each teacher has the responsibility for logging attendance and absences for each of the class periods. This type of student documentation will protect the teachers, the students, and keep the parents informed that the child is or is not in school on any given day.

Teachers who allow students to log student absences or presences are setting themselves up for a potential liable situation. If a student is marked present and that student is absent, and the student gets involved in an accident when the student should have been in school, the teacher doesn't have a defense, since the records will show that the attendance records were not accurate. Another fact to remember is the attendance records are the basis of a funding formula from the State Department of

Education to the school district and related to school attendance.

Scenario: *Teacher A allows student C to mark attendance in homeroom at the beginning of the school day. Student C Marks Student G present, but student G is actually absent. Student G doesn't appear on the absentee list which is available the 2nd hour of the day. The third hour teacher, notices that student G is not present in class; marks student G absent and marks the appropriate box for skipping class. The principal's office makes a call to student's home and informs the parent that their child is skipping 3rd period class. The parent informed the person making the call that her son is in the E.R. facility as a result of being hit by a car on the way to school.* (Who's in trouble?)

This scenario should never take place in the schools, but unfortunately it can and does happen when teachers give students the responsibility of checking attendance. This type of irresponsibility can impact a student's grade, result in a truancy issue, and furthermore, cause anxiety and stress for parents who release children to the care of school personnel. It can also result in a teacher losing their job for falsifying official school records.

Many schools receive part of the funding based upon the Average Daily Attendance (ADA) of students, which is another reason that teachers should not entrust this responsibility to students. Therefore, a school district loses a percentage of the funding for each student marked absent each day of the school term. The state periodically audits the school attendance records to check for discrepancies that could or might occur such as mentioned in the above scenario. Subsequently, an audit may correct an attendance error, but will not correct the liability error of the teacher.

Curriculum Issues

School administrators and teachers are responsible for the changing of the guard when it comes to academic standards and assessment relating to student achievement. Federal mandated legislation set standards for schools to reach in "closing the achievement gap". Along with the standards were penalties for not meeting the benchmarks, such as loss of federal funds, parents allowed to transfer their child to another school, or even worse, a school being forced to close and reorganize.

Schools are required to teach certain mandated curricula and it is the teachers' responsibility to deliver the instructional process. The responsibility of determining public school curricula is left to individual states, which is determined through legislation. It is required of local boards of education to offer those courses required by state statute. [21]

Occasionally parents will refuse to allow the child to take a particular course. This is an area where school administrators must be cautious in the decision making process. For example, a case in Alabama, a female student refused to take a physical education class on the grounds that it was against the child's religious belief not to dress in an immoral way before others. Even though the school made accommodations for altering the required dress, the parents sued the school board of education. The court held for the district. [22]

As long as the constitutional rights of students are not violated, the courts will invariably side with the local school districts when curricular issues are involved. If the states don't require through statute, that a student is entitled to a specific course of study, then students have no property right to be admitted to any specific course of study. [24]

The No Child Left Behind Act was enacted into law in 2003 and signed by President Bush. Although the Constitution was written to leave the responsibility of educating children to the individual states, this law gave a new meaning to the federal government's role in public education by instilling rewards and sanctions for outcomes and performances.

Teachers are receiving the brunt of this law as they are expected to bring all students to the specified level or exceeding the level set forth in the annual objectives. In other words, teachers are accountable for students' academic performance to close the achievement gap. [25]

Instructional Time

Most states have a mandated amount of instructional time required for students to receive in a school day. Kentucky, for example, requires a six-hour instructional day. [24] What does this mean for teachers? A new teacher or administrator must be aware of the policies and statutes of the school district and the state of their employment. An excuse, "I didn't know the rules" won't sustain school personnel in the court of laws. Preparing and following adequate lesson plans for each subject taught and maintaining accurate records of students' assignments and test scores can be a good defense in an alleged malpractice suit.

Educational malpractice litigation has not been very successful in the majority of cases filed. Parents are required to have the children in school on a regular basis, and their expectations are for the school to provide for a safe learning environment. [26] Teachers who forfeit or ignore their professional obligation to provide such a classroom environment, fail to follow the lesson plans, teach the core content, and monitor student progress, set themselves up for the litigation process. If the building administrator hasn't documented the necessary observation/evaluation forms, that administrator will be a party of the litigation process.

Another malpractice case, *Donohue v. Copiague Union Free School District in New York, a parent sued on the basis of the child "lacking rudimentary ability to comprehend written English on a level sufficient to enable him to complete applications for employment."* [27] Even though the court held in favor of the school district, the case, as in any case against a school district, established a mindset of distrust by many, toward public school education.

Bullying and Harassment

It is a known fact that bullying is a significant problem in every school system in the country. In those districts when it is said that the district does not have a bullying problem, the leadership must have their "heads in the sand". Some children and youth face this terrible and treacherous behavior on a daily basis and are afraid to report this to the teachers or administration.

> *"Bullying is using unwanted, aggressive behavior that involves a real or perceived power imbalance towards another person. The behavior is repeated, or has the potential to be repeated, over time".* [28]

> *"There are three types of bullying. Verbal bullying is saying or writing mean things, such as teasing, name-calling, making*

*inappropriate sexual comments, taunting,
or threatening to cause
harm. Social/relational bullying involves
hurting someone's reputation or
relationships, such as leaving someone out
on purpose, telling other children not to be
friends with someone, spreading rumors
about someone, and embarrassing
someone in public. Physical
bullying involves hurting a person's body or
possessions, such as hitting, kicking,
pinching, spitting, tripping, pushing, taking
or breaking someone's things, and making
mean or rude hand gestures." [29]*

Teacher, principals, and other administrators must be aware that a bullying problem exists and develop the school culture where this kind of behavior will not be tolerated. Students who are bullied should feel free to report the incident(s) without the feeling of reprisal. Where school leaders permit bullying to occur, without taking the necessary steps to stop it, grave consequences could befall the school district from the teacher, principal, superintendent and the board of education. Therefore, it is incumbent on all school leaders to have policies in place and carried out in a manner that will stop "bullying in its tracks".

The Kentucky Legislature in March, 2016 passed SB 228 that requires all school districts in Kentucky to develop policies on school bullying. This law specifically requires districts to alter student codes of conduct to enhance their efforts to address and to reduce bullying.

Copyright Issues

The experiences as professional educators lead one to believe that the issues of copyright violations are ignored by many educators, especially classroom teachers. Whether it is the lack of understanding of the copyright law or the attitude, "I won't get caught," the end result is the same, i.e., it is a violation, and it can cost the violator.

There is a principle of "fair use" which allows a person to use some copyright material without permission. The "fair use" concept was incorporated into the 1976 revisions of the Copyright Act. [30] But one must be cautious in overusing and abusing the "fair use" principle. Before deciding to make copies of someone else's material, certain guidelines must be considered:

The amount of work (volume) to be copied; was the work created to be sold; does copying the work cut into the author's ability to profit from the work?

Copyrighting can be considered as modern day piracy and should be respected as such. Teachers are not exempt from the copyright law. A case that came before the Ninth Circuit Court of Appeals involved a teacher who duplicated a copyrighted booklet to be used as a learning packet for students. This was an <u>abridgment of the copyright</u>

law. [31]

As the amount of computer software increased over the years and the abuse that followed, Congress amended the copyright law to include computer software. [32] Teachers should check with their district technology director before copying programs, videos, movies, etc.

Endnotes:

1. Kentucky School Board *ENews Service, Oct. 2008.*
2. *Gammon v. Edwardsville*, 403N.E.2d 43 (Ill.App. 1980).
3. *Libby v. West Coast Rock co., Inc.*, 308 So.2d 602 (Fla.App.1975)
4. *Titus v.* Lindberg, 49 N.J. 66, 228 A.2d 65 (1967)
5. Kentucky Revised Statute 160.295; Kentucky Administrative Regulation 704 KAR 7.050
6. Fifth Amendment of the United States Constitution
7. Kentucky Statute: KRS 160.295
8. *Ingraham v. Wright*, 430 U.S. 651, 97 S.Ct. 1401, 51 L.Ed.2d.711 (1977)
9. *Citation: Gottlieb v. Laurel Highlands School District,* 3rd U.S. Circuit Court of Appeals, No. 00-3422 (2001)
10. *Kearney, Christopher A. Casebook in Child Behavior Disorder, 3rd Ed. Thomas Wadsworth, U.S.2006.*
11. *Citation: Britton v. Marquette Circuit Court, Court appeals of Michigan,* No. 225883 (2001).
12. *LaMorte, Michael W., School Law, Cases and Concepts,* 6th ed. Allyn & Bacon, Boston. (19
13. *Raleigh v. Independent School District No. 625, 275 N.W.2d 572 Minn. (1979).*
14. KRS 620.040(5)(c).
15. *Garcia v. Miera*, 817 F.2d 650 (10th Cir. 1987).
16. Dunklee, Dennis R. and Shoop, Robert J., The Principal's Quick Reference guide to School Law. *Reducing liability, Litigation, and other Potential Legal Tangles. 2nd.* Corwin Press, California. (2006).
17. *King v. Kartenson*, 720 S.W.2d 65 (Tenn App.

66

1986).

18. *Marcantel v. Allen Parish School Board,* 490 So.2d 1162 (La.APP.3d Cir.1986).
19. *Partin v. Vernon Parish School Board.* 343 So.2d 417 (La .Appeals Ct., 1977).
20. McCarthy, Martha M. & Cambron=McCabe, Nelda H. Public School Law. *Teachers and Student Rights, 3rd ed..* Allyn and Bacon, Boston. (1992).
21. *Pierce v. Society of Sisters 268 U.S. 510, 535 (1925)*
22. *KRS 159. No Pass, No Drive Statute for the State of Kentucky.*
23. MCarthy, Martha M. and Cambron-McCabe, Nelda H. Public School Law. *Teachers' and Students' Rights. Allyn and Bacon.* Boston, 1987.
24. *Mitchell v. McCall,* 143 So. 2d 629 (Alabama, 1962).
25. *No Child Left Behind Act. (2001)*
26. *KRS 158. 060- Kentucky Revised Statute (2008)*
27. *Peter W. v. San Francisco Unified School District,* 131 Cal. Rptr. 854 (Cal. Ct. App. 1976).
28. *17 U.S.C. & 101 et seq, (1988).*
29. Stopbullying.gov., *Published: 1/8/2016 8:28 A.M.*
30. *Ibid.*
31. *Donohue v. Copiague Union Free School District, 391 N.E.2d 1352 (N.Y. 1979).*
32. *Marcus v. Rowley, 695 F.2d 1171 (9th Cir. 1983).*
33. *Ibid.*

Additional Court Cases:

1. *Ingram v. Wright,* 430 U.S. 651 (1977).
2. *Wise v. Pea Ridge School district, #109, 675 E.Supp. 1524 (W,D, Ark. 1987).*
3. *Gasperson v. Harnett County Board of Education,* 330 S.E.2d 489 (N.C. App. 1985).
4. Gonyaw v. Gray, 361 F.Sup. 366 (D.Vt. 1973).
5. *People v. DeCaro,* 308 N.E.2d 196 (Ill.App.1st District,1974).
6. *Stretter v. Hundley*, 580 S.W.2d 283 (Mo. 1979).
7. *17 U.S.C. 117(1988).*
8. *Arundar v. Dekalb County School Dist.,* 620 F.2d 493 (5th Cir. 1980).

Chapter Five – FREEDOM OF EXPRESSION

Speech

Of all the freedoms guaranteed in this country, none is more protected than the right of freedom of speech.

The First Amendment to the Constitution provides that guarantee. This part of the Constitution has provoked numerous court cases involving students' and teachers' rights to freedom of expression. [1]

The first amendment rights of students may be restricted based upon the types of expressions and the effect the expressions will have on the school climate. Students or teachers do have some limitations to their constitutional rights of freedom of speech or expression upon entering the school. This is due to the rules and laws that govern the school surroundings.

For example, Fox News reported that a kindergarten teacher in an Indiana elementary school berated one of the students on a regular basis. The father of the kindergarten student placed a tape recorder in the child's pocket and when this type of unethical behavior toward the child happened again, it was documented. The kindergarten teacher was suspended and the parents of the child are considering litigation against the teacher, the principal and the school district. This could have been avoided had the teacher been provided information on the "pitfalls" of negative expressions to students. [2]

It is important for teachers to understand that their conduct is open to scrutiny at all times and can become skeletons in the closet. Considering the consequences of one's behavior in any forum should always be a priority.

Maintaining a professional code of ethics and constant awareness of how one projects self in conversation and/or by body language can reduce the potential of breaching the First Amendment.

Teachers and administrators have a responsibility to provide a classroom environment that is free from bullying, coercion, harassment, and one which is conducive to learning and achievement. It is also their responsibility to model respect, to honor and protect student's individual rights. Talking "down" to a student or behaving in an unprofessional manner toward students can quickly create a barrier for learning, and possibly put an educator's career in jeopardy.

As mentioned previously, student and teacher expression can have limited First Amendment protection. Obscene, defamatory, and inflammatory expression are not protected by the First Amendment. Material, to be classified obscene, must violate three tests developed by the U. S. Supreme Court: (1)" It must appeal to the prurient or lustful interest of minors, (2) it must describe sexual conduct in a way that is "potently offensive" to community standards, and (3) taken as a whole, it "must lack serious literary, artistic, political or scientific value." [3]

In 1972, a non-tenured teacher's contract was not renewed on the following grounds:

- "Belittling instructions given by the principal in the presence of the teaching staff.

- Advising faculty members that the principal had failed to give instructions on attendance to a rally. (This advice was false.)

- Requesting at a staff meeting that the teacher be given the right to criticize the principal over the intercom system to all classrooms.

- Entering the classroom of another teacher and creating embarrassment to the teacher before the students.

- Questioning the authority of the principal to remove aides from classroom and library, and behaving in an insubordinate manner to the principal.

- Making threat of physical harm to an administration official before other personnel."

This was the contents of the letter sent to the

teacher from the Rowan County Superintendent of Schools in Morehead, Ky. The teacher did admit to the charges of (1), (3), (4), and (5), on the grounds of freedom of expression. The teacher also made physical contact with the superintendent by shoving the superintendent in the presence of a teacher colleague, and stated that the principal and superintendent were unfit for their positions. As per the court case, the teacher had made a statement, "someone ought to kill him", and the teacher "would lay a .38 between his eyes," and that both administrators "ought to be shot." (4)

Are the teachers behavior and expressions constitutionally protected by the First Amendment? Were the First Amendment rights of the teacher debased?

The landmark Pickering case in Illinois gave credence to the First Amendment. Marvin Pickering taught high school in Joliet, Illinois, and wrote a letter to the editor of the local paper criticizing the School Board of Education on how funds were being allocated between education and the athletic programs. Mr. Pickering wrote the letter after the citizens defeated a proposed tax increase and in the letter supported the tax increase but exaggerated the amount the school board was spending on athletics. As the result of Mr. Pickering's letter to the paper, he was fired by the school board. Mr. Pickering challenged the dismissal in court and was vindicated by the Supreme Court on the grounds that Mr. Pickering's interests were based on public interests where issues such as these should be open to public debate. [5]

If the school district could have proven that Mr. Pickering's remarks resulted in "bad blood" among the staff and administrators that negatively impacted the learning environment, then Mr. Pickering would have been "times gone by." [6]

Since the *Pickering* case, teachers have aggressively challenged school boards' decisions on certain disciplinary actions and dismissals on grounds that those teachers were protected under the First Amendment and sometimes the Fourteenth Amendment.

Fred Doyle, a non-tenured teacher in Ohio, decided to make a telephone call to the local radio station criticizing a new policy on teacher grooming. Mr. Doyle was not a teacher "exemplar", and had several other incidents which had been written up and had been reprimanded by the principal of the school. Subsequently, and not surprising, Mr. Doyle's contract was not renewed for the upcoming school year. Mr. Doyle sued on the grounds that the speech to the radio station was protected. Although, the trial court and Sixth Circuit Court of Appeals held in Mr. Doyle's reinstatement appeal, based upon protected expression, the Supreme Court ruled in favor of dismissal based upon the "other incidents" that were unbecoming of a teacher.

The "other incidents" referred to in the Doyle case were: (a) getting into an argument with employees of the school cafeteria regarding the food which had been served; (b) referred to students that had been disciplined as "sob(s)."; and (c) made obscene gestures toward female students for not following the teacher's supervision rules in the lunchroom. [7]

Considering the charges against Mr. Doyle, were his constitutional rights violated? Should the obscene gestures be constitutionally protected? Was the board's decision to non-renew Doyle's contract appropriate?

In the case of *Givhan v. Western Line Consolidated School District, a teacher was dismissed for privately expressing complaints and opinions to the principal of the school. This teacher was exonerated on **the grounds that teachers do not forfeit their protection against** governmental abridgement of freedom of speech by expressing their opinions privately.* [8]

When a high school coach was suspended for making reference to the team as cowards in an interview by a local reporter the coach sued the school board stating that it was the coach's freedom of speech that had been violated. The suspension was overruled in a court decision on the basis that those comments made were not a matter of public concern. [9]

Teachers are faced with many issues and mandates for which there has been no opportunity for input. Teachers are constantly reminded that that their jobs can be on the line if students do not reach the performance benchmarks set by state and federal government reform acts. For instance, a penalty embedded within the *"No Child Left Behind Act"* allows parents to move their children to another school if their own school falls below expected and required levels of performance. The fallout from the above scenario could result in a reduction of staff, public support of the school, or worse, closing of the school.

Political issues and poor judgment made by administrators can result in causing staff to voice their opinions negatively as employees and not as concerned citizens regarding their work place. If the comments are interpreted as slanderous toward their organization or a person, they may not be protected by the First Amendment. Therefore, it is imperative that teachers and administrators understand their limitations of freedom of expression relating to their position. [10]

During the case of *Gilbertson v. McAlister,* the court outlined some valuable guidelines for educators to consider and follow, to stay within the boundaries of the First Amendment and out of court:

- *The impact on harmony, personal loyalty and confidence among co-workers.*

- *The degree of falsity of statements.*

- *The place where speech or distribution of material occurred.*

- *The impact of the staff and students, and*

- *The degree to which the teacher's conduct lacked professionalism.* (11)

It is important to know that the Court through the first amendment has given schools much leeway in the employment of expression by its' students and staff, but these rights must receive "scrupulous" protection "if we are not to strangle the free mind at its source and teach youth to discount important principles of the government as mere platitudes".(12) The schools, under the protection of the first amendment have always been considered as "a market place of ideas" and for a "robust exchange of ideas" and is "a special concern of the first amendment."(13)

As employers and employees, including teachers, considering correcting or assessing

*the legitimacy of an "expression," a
determination must be made whether the
communication expresses an idea relative to the
appropriate forum in which it is delivered and
does it meet the intent of the first amendment
(14). An example would be if a student or fellow
worker cried out, "a terrorist has just entered the
building!" (15)*

As schools are becoming more global the
culture is rapidly becoming more vulnerable to
change in "small community" values and mores.
Educators, specifically, are being challenged on
how to address obscene, vulgar and
inflammatory expressions by students.   The
Supreme Court issued the following guidelines
to help address this growing issue:

- "Whether "the average person, applying
  contemporary community standards: would find
  that the work, taken as a whole, appeals to the
  prurient interest....

- Whether the work depicts or describes, in a
  patently offensive way, sexual conduct
  specifically defined by the applicable state law;
  and

- Whether the work, taken as a whole, lacks
  serious literary, artistic, political or scientific
  value." (16)

Although these guidelines appeared to be

geared toward literary works, obscene types of expression should not be acceptable or tolerated in the workplace. The courts have upheld cases involving obscene language directed toward educators. A case in Louisiana, involved a student who was recommended for expulsion because of the student's inflammatory, indecent and threatening language toward a teacher. The court ruled in favor of the school district. [17] In the state of Pennsylvania, a student took the liberty of expression too far when using indecent remarks toward the teacher who was in a shopping mall. [18]

The libraries in public schools have been targeted because of the First Amendment violation. A group of students protested against the school removing reading materials such as the Island Trees and other questionable literary works which contained "offensive "and unacceptable passages. One of the students, Francis Pico sued the School Board, resulting in the Supreme Court ruling on behalf of the students and took the point of view that because administrators did not agree with the content of books, it was not justifiable to remove the material from the school library. [19]

Endnotes:

1. *U. S. Constitution, Articles I, II, III, ratified 1798.*
2. *Fox News, May 2008.*
3. *Lunenburg and Ornstein, 2008.*
4. *Amburgey v. Rowan County Board of Education*
5. McCarthy, Marha M., & Cambron-McCabe, Nelda H. Public School Law. *Teachers and Students' Rights.3ʳᵈ ed. Allyn and Bacon, Mass. (1992).*
6. *Pickering v. Board of Education,* 391 U.S. 563 (1968)
7. *Doyle v. Mt. Healthy City School District,* 670 F.2d 59 (6ᵗʰ Cir. 1982).
8. *Givhan v. Western Line Consolidated School District,* 439 U.S. 410 (1979
9. *Brayton v. Monson Public Schools,* 950 F. Supp. 33 (Mass. 1997).
10. *Essex, Nathan L. A Teacher*'s Pocket Guide to School Law. Allyn and Bacon
11. *Gilbertson v. McAlister, 403, F.Supp. 1 (D. Conn. 1975).*
12. *West Virginia Board of Education v. Barnette,* 319 U.S. 624,637 (1934).
13. *Keyishian v. Board of Regents,* 385, U.S., 589, 603 (1967), partial quoting.
14. *Jarman v. Williams, 753 F.2d, 8ᵗʰ Circuit Ct., 1955).*
15. *Schneck v. United States, 249 U.S. 47, 52 (1919).*
16. 413. U.S. 15, 24 (1973).
17. *Williams v. Turner,* 382 So 2d 1040 (La. Ct.App. 1980).
18. *Fenton v. Stear, 423 F. Supp. 767, 771 (W,D, Pa, 1976).*
19. *Board of Education v. Pico ,457 U.S, 853, 638 F.2d 404 (1982)*

Additional Court Cases:

1. Shelton v. Tucker, 364 U.S. 479,487 (1960),
2. United States v. Associated Press, 52 F. Supp. 362, 372 (S.D.N.Y. (1943).
3. *Thompkins v. Vikers,* 26 F.32 603 (5th Cir. 1994).
4. *Tardif v. Quinn,* 545 F.2d 761 (1s Cir. 1976).
5. Kern Alexander and M.David Alexander, *American Public School Law* St. Paul, Minnesota, West, (2001).
6. *Elfbrandt v. Russell,* 384 U.S. 11 (1966)

Chapter Six – TEACHERS AS EXEMPLARS

This is an area of teacher professionalism and expectations that may vary from state to state and community to community depending upon what is viewed as acceptable exemplary conduct for teachers. Since this country has been divided, politically, into red and blue states, or conservative and liberal, depending on one's point of reference and life style, it is supposed that an individual could or should select their place of reference accordingly. All humor aside, educators in particular must have a strong code of ethics and character if teachers are to be a positive role model for their students. School boards and state departments of education should not have to mandate the type of conduct for educators to exhibit. For example, in 1915 in West Virginia, a particular school board had a set of rules for teachers to follow:

a) "You are not to marry during the term of your contract".
b) You are not to keep company with men.
c) You must be home between the hours of 8:00 p.m. and 6:00 a.m. unless attending a school function.
d) You may not loiter downtown in ice cream stores.
e) You may not travel beyond city limits unless you have the permission of the

chairman of the board.

f) You may not ride in a carriage or automobile with any man unless he is your father or brother.

g) You may not smoke cigarettes.

h) You may not dress in bright colors.

i) You may under no circumstances dye your hair.

j) You must wear at least two petticoats.

k) Your dresses must not be any shorter than two inches above the ankle.

l) To keep the schoolroom neat and clean, you must sweep the floor at least once daily; scrub the floor at least once a week with hot, soapy water; clean the blackboard at least once a day, and start the fire at 7:00 a.m. so the room will be warm by 8:00 a.m. "[1]

As one thinks about the term exemplar, many definitions may come to mind. For those who are parents, there is one's own expectations of the type of role model that is expected of teachers or day care workers. Perhaps one might focus on dress, hair style, grooming, professionalism, morality, etc. Teachers and administrators cannot and will not satisfy all of the stakeholders, but must be aware and understand the culture in their community. It is also important that educators understand the moral and ethical expectations associated with that culture. These expectations usually vary from region to region, metropolitan areas to rural, etc.

It is important that administrators and teachers try to match their definition of exemplar with the customs, culture and traditions of the community in their place of employment. If a teacher's and/or administrators' values are in conflict with the mores of the geographical area of their employment, this could result in a game of Russian roulette with their career.

Moral turpitude, unfitness, conduct unbecoming of a teacher and immorality are grounds for teacher dismissal. With this in mind, some consideration should be given to the following questions:

- Will the teacher's behavior or conduct result in destroying a career, a child's life, and spending time prison time?

- Will the teacher's behavior or conduct have a direct impact on the teacher's performance or students' performance in the classroom?

- Will the teacher's behavior or conduct affect the relationship with colleagues?

- Will the teacher's behavior or conduct result in a negative public view toward the school district?

  Regardless of the age of the educators and the students, inappropriate contact or sexual innuendos should never occur with students. Inappropriate sexual behavior with young people has been the demise of many adults and educators. A middle school teacher in Harlan County, Kentucky, was arrested and escorted out of the class due to crossing the line with students. The mother of a young middle school girl who happened to be a student of this teacher opened the diary of the daughter's while cleaning up the student's room at home. The contents of the journal were very graphic and shocking. The young girl had documented sexual encounters with the teacher. The mother contacted law enforcement who, after their investigation of the alleged encounters, arrested the teacher who is now serving prison time.

Not a week goes by without a public school educator or an adult who has allegedly "crossed the line" with students or young people in a sexually, or inappropriate manner. The trauma associated with the allegations, whether the person is guilty or innocent, can be a painful and an emotional issue to endure. The allegation itself can damage one's reputation and professional career.

Educators should never lose sight of the main focus of their role to help provide a protective shield for young people under their supervision. The public expects educators to be exemplary in their conduct and to exhibit behavior above that behavior expected of the average citizen. The Pennsylvania Supreme Court defined immorality as "a course of conduct as offends the morals of the community and is a bad example to the youth whose ideals of a teacher is supposed to be fostered and elevated." [2]

The Supreme Court of Pennsylvania set the benchmark for teachers being exemplar in the case of *Horosko v. School District of Mr. Pleasant* in 1939.[3] "It has always been the recognized duty of the teacher to conduct one's self in such a way as to command the respect and good will of the community.

It can happen after what appears to be a very innocent gesture or comment for a teacher or administrator to get caught in the web of immorality and inappropriateness. The courts have no patience when dealing with teachers who cross the line of being sexually inappropriate with students. In the case of *Fadler v. Illinois State Board of Education, the teacher was fired when he positioned his hands inside the jeans of a female student on the buttocks; on other occasions he fondled the breasts of a female student.* [4]

"Education has always regarded the example set by the teacher as of great importance...." [5] A quick way to end a career in the teaching profession is getting sexually inappropriate with students, whether it is verbally or physical. [6]

Enough court cases involving immorality of teachers have sent a clear message that educators cannot hide behind their constitutional privacy rights for protection for being sexually involved or inappropriate with students. The following case scenarios are examples of teachers who have taken advantage of their influence with students in unacceptable and inappropriate ways:

- A teacher in Pennsylvania was dismissed when the teacher began "playing" up to a student who was sixteen. The teacher's gestures included giving gifts and writing notes of romance on the chalk board and other "innocent come-on's." The student tried to ignore the teacher's overtures, but the teacher was insistent that a relationship begin even though the student was resisting the advances. [7]

- A fourth grade teacher's inappropriate behavior toward two students where one was a student in the class. The male teacher was living with the girl's divorced mother and while the mother was undergoing medical treatment in the hospital for a month, the teacher's immoral conduct began. The sisters slept in the same bed. The male teacher touched their breasts, took nude photographs of the girls and would parade around them in the nude. [8] **This is**

absolutely repulsive, but it happened.

- A high school teacher in the state of Washington was dismissed when the teacher partied with two female students in the teacher's house, serving them alcoholic drinks, and undressing one of the students when the student became over intoxicated and passed out. [9]

The following court cases may cause educators to have second thoughts before they get themselves entrapped in a sexual situation of no return: A junior high school counselor was terminated for serious breaches of professional ethics which involved wagering weight-loss bets with a couple of 9th grade students. It wasn't the bets that did the counselor in, even though this was unethical, it was the sexual activities with the students. The counselor was also administering oral surveys to students relating to their sexual participation and then breaching student's confidentiality from the information received. [10]

In Iowa, a teacher was dismissed after a student admitted that the student was having sexual intercourse with one of the teachers. [11] A high school drama teacher in Michigan was also dismissed after taking a two-week trip with the student. The teacher had been seen kissing the student and laying around with the student on a mattress. [12]

In 1986 the Hopkins County Board of Education "terminated the contracts of the Woods brothers for conduct unbecoming of a teacher for immoral conduct involving off-campus activities with students, notwithstanding written records indicating satisfactory teacher performance. The teachers were discharged for off-campus smoking of marijuana with two fifteen-year-old female students." This case was referred to the Kentucky Supreme Court which held for the Hopkins County Board of Education. [13]

The teaching profession occupies a position of public trust involving not only the individual teacher's personal conduct, but also the interaction of the school and the community. Education is most effective when these relationships operate in a friendly, cooperative, and constructive manner. A teacher's conduct should meet acceptable standards of the community, be in compliance with the law and show respect to the rights of others.

In the case of *Kirpatrick v. Wright,* the teacher argued vehemently that since the courts were indecisive on the definition of immorality, the sexual conduct allegation with a student should not be permissible in court because of the vagueness of the definition of immorality.[14] A teacher in the State of Washington was found guilty of having sex with a minor. The Appeals

Court made a determination that this conduct of the teacher was harmful to the school district. [15] Is this a surprise?

On Tuesday, June 3, 2008, Fox News reported that teachers were on "YouTube" showing provocative poses that were sexual in nature, for example, showing tattoos on breasts, drinking alcohol from a teacher's belly button, and making sexual comments.

These comments and poses may not be illegal. Boards of education in most cases will say this is "behavior unbecoming of a teacher;" whereby the teacher could be suspended or fired. Educators must be mindful of the fact that unacceptable provocative behavior can end up on YouTube, Facebook or Myspace. Many students who are skilled in the latest technology will be glad to oblige without the teacher's knowledge.

Some of the other embarrassing news items that came across Fox News which help drive home the point this book is attempting to make are:

- "In Virginia, high school art teacher was fired after posting photos of his "butt art" on the Web, which were viewed by scores of students. The budding artist applied paint to the teacher's posterior and genitalia, which was then pressed onto canvases. With the help of the ACLU, the teacher sued the school district last fall claiming a violation of his First Amendment rights.

- The band director from Broward County, Florida, was dismissed after school officials viewed the teacher's Myspace profile that included rambling about sex, drugs, and depression.

- A Colorado English teacher lost the teaching job after composing and posting sexually explicit poetry on the Myspace site. This exhibition was so graphic, that law enforcement was called in to investigate.

- A Nashville teacher was removed from teaching after posting "racy pictures" of herself, along with candid photos of the students, on Myspace.

- Another middle school teacher in Florida was terminated because of "offensive" and "unacceptable" photos and information on the Myspace page.

- In Massachusetts a teacher was suspended for Myspace postings including "sexually suggestive" photographs, videos of drinking alcohol, and references to women as "whores."

- A teacher assistant in Massachusetts was fired from the job because of Myspace postings. MTA represented the teacher assistant in arbitration and was successful in getting reinstatement with back pay, seniority and benefits. The arbitrator did conclude, that because of teacher's unprofessional misconduct, some form of discipline was warranted, which i.e. was determined to be a three-day suspension. Was justice served?

- But the clueless award goes to an Atlanta-area high school football coach who was forced to resign for storing on the school computer, photos of the assistant principal dressed in lingerie and posing in sexually suggestive ways. The photos were discovered by a student who the coach had asked to work on the computer. The student not only took the liberty of posting the photos on the Internet but shared them with other students at the school.

- Last October, reporters for The Columbus Dispatch conducted an investigation of Myspace profiles posted by Ohio teachers. The newspaper quoted one 25-year-old teacher bragging about being "an aggressive freak in bed," "sexy," and "an outstanding kisser." Another teacher wrote on a page about recent exploits such as: "gotten drunk," "taken drugs," and "gone skinny-dipping."[16]

"In the wake of these reports, the Ohio Education Association urged all OEA members to remove any personal profiles previously posted on Myspace or Facebook. The Association also warned members those profiles "can be used as evidence in disciplinary proceedings," which could "affect not only a teacher's current job but their teaching license" as well." [17]

Blogging has become a contemporary forum for people to voice their opinion, criticize their organization or supervisor, or push the limits of the First Amendment of the United States Constitution. Professionals should be extremely cautious in utilizing technology for questionable types of communication. It is a source of documentation that can be incriminating.

While the courts have not yet decided any of these teacher blogging cases, it's the general rule that school employees can be disciplined for off-duty conduct if the school district can show that the conduct had an adverse impact on the school or the teacher's ability to teach. It would not be difficult for an attorney to introduce an immoral charge involving sexually explicit scenes or other inappropriate content by educators which is viewed on YouTube, My space, and other hi-tech media forums

Different Life Style
This text has addressed culture, community values and mores which impact or influence the expectations that educators should model for the students in their charged to teach and supervise. Therefore, it is paramount that school leaders address the issue of different life styles among the educator's ranks. The point is not to condone or promote, but to provide guidelines to protect the educator whose sexual orientation might be problematic in affecting the work environment and students.

The main focus of this text is to provide a safety net for the employee and to increase the awareness of protecting students and children from any type of harm and/or abuse. The main concern is that all educators and employees conduct themselves in a proper manner so that "their behavior doesn't transgress or exceed school authorities or a community's zone of acceptance."[20]

The Constitution does afford certain amount of sexual conduct privacy outside the school workplace, but there are some limitations to the Privacy Act. One cannot choose any lifestyle if the lifestyle impinges adversely on students.

Having a different life style has been an area of contention in relations to freedom of expression and privacy. Courts have been divided on this issue as to whether this lifestyle impacts a teacher's effectiveness and therefore making the teacher unfit to be in the classroom with students. [21]

In California, for example, the Supreme Court declared that a teacher's sexual orientation itself does not justify the teacher being dismissed, but the behavior resulting to moral turpitude, an immoral act, must be related to the teacher being unfit to teach. [22]

A school board doesn't have the right to terminate employment of an employee on the grounds that the board does not agree with the employee's particular life style. There must be a connection between the educator's lifestyle and fitness to teach or whether the lifestyle has adverse effect on the students' behavior and academic performance.

Another California case involved a male teacher who made sexual advances toward a plain-clothes police officer observing the breach. The teacher's certification was revoked and his employment was terminated. [23] In the case of *Gaylord v. Tacoma School District* in the State of Washington, a teacher who was open about the teacher's homosexual lifestyle was dismissed from employment. The teacher was an exemplary teacher with twelve years of experience. The lifestyle was considered immoral and not meeting the norms and values expected by the school board and the society. Keep in mind, the year was 1977. This was an era that homosexuality was not acceptable by the majority of the public. Also, the teacher's colleagues and students were not comfortable around the teacher, thus creating a somewhat toxic work and learning climate. [24]

Since the term "fitness to teach" has been used, it is appropriate to define the expression. An appellate court in Illinois gave the definition of unfitness as "conduct detrimental to the operation of the school....." [25] Other areas that fall under the category of unfitness are physical, mental, and emotional disorders. Any disorder that incapacitates the ability of a teacher to perform duties as assigned can result in termination. [26]

Teachers with medical conditions that impair their ability to fulfill their duties on a regular basis are at risk of being terminated if the impairment is the result of not taking their medication as prescribed. If a teacher is diabetic and does not check the blood-sugar levels, this also places the teacher at risk of being a liability to the school which could result in termination. [27]

Conduct and Association

Teachers are required to be familiar with and abide by all local, state and federal laws, administrative regulations as well as the policies and decisions of the School Board.

Teachers shall be expected to observe at least the following standards of conduct that are outlined in many Board of Education Policies:

- Be courteous to students, one another, and the public, and present oneself in a professional and ethical manner.

- Recognize and respect the rights and property of students, other employees, and the public.

- Maintain confidentiality of all matters relating to students and other employees.

- Demonstrate dependable attendance and punctuality with regard to assigned activities and work schedules.

- Observe and adhere to all terms of an employee's contract or job description.

- Strive to keep current and knowledgeable about the employee's area of responsibility.

- Refrain from using undue influence to gain, or attempt to gain, promotion, leave, favorable assignments, or other individual benefit or advantage.

- Advocate positive personal behavior on or off campus and attempt to avoid improprieties or the appearance of improprieties." [28]

Endnotes:

1. Lamont, Michael W. School Law, *Cases and Concepts.* 6th Edition, Allyn and Bacon, Boston. 1999.(pg. 234).
2. *Horosko v. School District of Mt. Pleasant,* 6 A.2d 866, 868 (Pa. 1939), *cert. denied, 308* U.S. 553 (1939).
3. Ibid.
4. *Fadler v. Illinois State Board of Education, 153 Illinois. App.32 1024, 106 Illnois. 840 506 N.E. 2d 640 (5 District, 1987).*
5. *Strain v. Rapid City School Board,* 447 N.W.2d 332 (S.D. 1989).
6. *Keeting v. Riverside Board of School Directors,* 513 A.2d 547 (Pa. Commonwealth, 1986).
7. *Lile v. Hancock Place School District,* 701 S.W.2d 500 (Mo.App.1985).
8. *Couperville School District, No. 204 v. Vivian,* 677 P2d 192 (Washington App. 1984).
9. McCarthy, Martha M. and Cambron-McCabe, Nelda N. Public School Law, *Teachers and students' Rights.* 3rd Edition, Allyn & Bacon, Boston, 1992
10. *Downie v. Indep. School district.* No. 141, 367N.W.2d 913 (Minnesota
    a. *App. 1985).)*
11. *Libe v. Board of Education,* 350 N.W.2d 748 (Iowa App. 1984).
12. *Clark v. Ann Arbor School Dist.,* 344 N.W.2d 48 (Mich.App/1983).
13. *Woods v. Board of Education of Hopkins County,* 717 S.W. (Kentucky, 1986).
14. *14 Kilpatrick v. Wright,* 437 F. Supp. 397, 399 (M.D. Alabama 1977).
15. *Denton v. south Kitsap School District.* No. 402, 516 P.2d (1980, Washington, Ct. App.,

1973).

16. Fox News, (June 2008)
17. Columbus Dispatch, (October 2007).
18. NEA Today, Rights watch, (April, 2008).
19. *Ibid.*
20. LaMorte, Michael, W. School Law, Cases and Concepts. 8th ed.
21. *Sherburne* v. School Board of Suwannee County, 455 SO.2d 1057 (Florida District Ct. App. 1984).
22. Morrison v. State Board of Education, 57 California Rptr. 69 (California Ct. App. 1967).
23. *Sarac v. State Board of Education,* 57 Cal. Rptr. 69 (California, Court of App. 1967).
24. *Gaylord v. Tacoma School District* No. 10, 559 P2d 1340 (Washington, 1977), *cert. denied,* 434 U.S. 870 (1977).
25. *Lombardo v. Board of Education School District, N0 27, 241 N.E.2d 495, 498 (Illinois App. Ct. 1968).*
26. *Fitzpatrick v. board of Education of the Mamaroneck Union Free School Dist., 465 N.Y.S.2d 240 (New York APP Div. 1983).*
27. *Smith v. Board of Education of Fort Madison Community School District, 293 N.W.2d 221 (Iowa, 1980).*
28. Kentucky School Board Association's Policy Manuel, (2008).

Additional Court Cases:

1. Acanfora v. Board of Education of Montgomery County, 491 F.2d 498 (4th Circuit Ct. 1971), cert. denied, 410 U.S. 836 (1977).
2. Board of Education of Long Beach Unified School District v. Jack M., 566 P.2d 602, California (1977).
3. Burton v. Cascade School District Union High School No. 5, 512 491F.2d 498 (4th Circuit, 9174)
4. Gish v. Board of Education of the Borough of Paramus, 366 A.2d 1337 (1977), cert. denied, 434 U.S. 879 (1977).
5. Morrison v. State Board of Education, 461 P.2d 375, California ((1969)

Chapter Seven – PRIVACY ISSUES

The Fourth Amendment to the Constitution provides an assurance that citizens will be secure in their persons, houses, papers, etc., against unreasonable searches and seizures without probable cause. On the other hand, the U.S. Supreme Court ruled that school officials could search students without adhering to the strict standard of "probable cause that is required by police officers or other law enforcement agencies. [1]

Search procedures must be initiated on the concept of reasonableness and the search must indicate a violation of school rules. This was a landmark case where two female students were observed by a teacher of smoking in the restroom. One of the girls confessed to smoking, but the other student denied smoking. The Associate Principal took the girls to the office and proceeded to open the purse of the girl who denied smoking. The process ended up with the Associate Principal going through all the contents of the student's purse after it was noticed that there was rolling paper. Several dollars in one girl's purse and a list of people who "owes her money" was visible. This matter was then turned over to the police. The parents sued on the basis of infringement of their daughter's privacy. The U.S. Supreme Court held in favor of the school, because the search was based upon reasonable suspicion. [2]

One must always take into consideration before making a search that there appears to be sufficient evidence or information to continue the search. The following questions also should be considered before making a search:

1. What is the proper way to proceed with the search?"

2. Does the evidence support a reasonable cause to perform the search?

3. Should law enforcement officials be involved in the search?

4. Should there be a witness to the search?

A middle school student was suspected of stealing a clock from the principal's office. An adult witness had seen the student in the office around the time the clock disappeared. The student was also seen with a bulky object protruding from his jacket. Incidentally, a pot of honey disappeared from the top of a microwave in the office area. The principal conducted a locker search of the student involved and found $3,000 worth of lunch tickets. Was the search legal? [3]

Proper or Improper search

In the case of *Cales v. Howell Public Schools*, a female student was in the parking lot and the security guard saw the female student acting rather suspiciously. The student was ordered to empty the purse she was carrying. In the student's possession was school admittance slips which had not been issued to that student. In the office the student was also told to take off the jeans and blouse in order for a female staff member to examine if anything was hidden in the bra. The search was justified by the assistant principal who had the belief that the student was in possession of drugs. The parents of the student sued the school district, naming the assistant principal for illegally conducting the search and violating the student's civil rights. The school district lost the suit and the assistant principal was not protected under governmental immunity. [4]

Another case illustrating improper search happened when a school bus driver observed two students on school grounds exchanging items. The driver thought it might be money and reported it to the principal. The principal and a teacher as a witness performed a "pat down" search. The search produced no evidence of drug paraphernalia. The students sued on the basis of the Fourth Amendment rights violation. The lower court disagreed, but the U.S. Court of Appeals ruled in favor of the students. [5]

Since 1994 when the federal government began requiring more rigid safety measures to stop and/or reduce the heinous crimes in the schools, the use of metal detectors became more common in many of the public schools. This legal method of intrusive search has reduced the number of tragedies with weapons by 50 percent in the nations' high schools, [6] and has also helped to decrease acts of vandalism on school property. [7]

It is essential that school personnel stay vigilant in keeping schools safe for students. Teachers must be cautious when undertaking a routine student search. It is necessary that they know the school board policy relating to student search, whether it be body search or personal item search. When in doubt, summon the principal of the school to make the decision. Educators must be sure that the source of information that might warrant a search is credible and reliable. Never search a student's locker without another staff member and the student present. All searches should involve a witness.

Endnotes:

1. DeskBook of Encyclopedia of American School Law. Data Research, Inc. (1989)
2. *New Jersey v. T.L.O.*, 105 S.Ct. 733 (1985)
3. *R.D.L. v. State*, 499 So.2d 31 (Fla.App.2d Dist.1986)
4. *Cales v. How Public Schools,* 635 F.Supp.454 (E.D.Mich, 1985)
5. *Biblrey v. Brown, 738 F.2d 1462 (9th Cir. 1984)*
6. *CNN Web Site, posted December, (1997).*
7. *Thompson v. Carthage School District, 87 F.3d 979, 89 Circuit Court, (1996).*

Additional Court Cases:

1. *DeRoches v. Caprio and School Board of Norfolk,* 156 f.3d 571, 129   Education L., Rep 628, 4th Cir. 1998).   This case involved searching a   student's backpack for stolen items.
2. *Isiah B. v. State of Wisconsin, 176 Wis.2d 639, 500 N.W.2d 637 (1993). (Locker search involving personal items.)*
3. *Kuehn v. Renton School District.* No. 403, 694 P.2d 1078 (Washington, 1985).
4. *Inier v. Lund*, 438 F.Supp.47 (N.D.N.Y.1977).
5. *Pica v. Wielgos,* 410 F.Supp. 1214 N.D. Ill. 1976).
6. *S.C. v. State*, 583, SC.2d 188, Miss. (1991).
7. *State v. Moore*, 254 N.J. Super 295, N.J. Super, App. Div. (1992).
8. *State v. Slattery, 56 Washington, App.820, Wash. Ct. App. (1990).*

Chapter Eight – CONFIDENTIALITY ISSUES

Beware, the teachers' lounge has been said to be the 'devil's workshop." This expression which has been around for some time may have some validity.

Educators need to be extremely cautious when discussing students' specific problems and their home life situation, other employees and their personal lives. It can be very easy to get entrapped into idle talk or gossip about a supervisor, fellow employee, a student, or parents.

One can enter into the venue of defamatory expression without the intention of doing harm to the third party. If this sort of communication is false or hear say and can be damaging to a person's reputation, it can be categorized as defamation or slander.

Name calling can come under this classification. For example, in Missouri, one of the teachers made the mistake of calling the two assistant principals "scabs". This incident took place while the teacher was on a picket line and felt that teachers were protected by the teachers' union.

The district, as a form of punishment to the teacher, began the transfer process to another school. Their rationale was not based on the exercise of freedom of speech. It was the teacher showing outward disrespect for supervisors which prompted the decision for the transfer. [1]

One must also be cautious of being overly critical of their supervisor in any forum. When criticism goes to the personal level, there could be liability generated, by the person leveling the criticism.

A high school principal decided to retaliate against the superintendent in a board meeting. The issue was that the principal's wife was transferred from one school to another. The criticism against the superintendent in the public forum was that a poor decision was made in with the transfer. The court upheld the district on the basis that this was a personal "beef" which did not impact the overall improvement of the school. [2]

Criticizing other teachers or employees can also result in unexpected repercussions. A teacher in Florida, while having a conference with the principal began an unsolicited questioning of some of the colleague's certification for the courses being taught, and it was expressed that the teacher present should be teaching the courses. As a result of that meeting and the teacher's criticism, the teacher was **reassigned** to teach elective courses. The teacher brought suit on the basis of the First Amendment Rights, but was not upheld in court because the comments were not public concern, but dealt with internal school policies and hiring practices. (3)

Students' records can be a volatile issue as far as protecting the privacy rights of students. (4) Schools have been ordered to delete erroneous information from students' school records.

When the Supreme Court ruled on *Griswold v. Connecticut,* the essence of this case was that one's personal privacy was guaranteed and protected by the Constitution. (5) Litigation brought against an Oklahoma School District because of irrelevant information placed in a student's permanent school files set the benchmark on what should or should not be entered in students' school files. The Supreme Court ordered that some of the information about a student be removed from the files. One entry in the file included a statement that a pupil had been "ruined by tobacco and alcohol." (6)

The *Family Educational Rights and Privacy Act (FERPA),* was enacted in 1974 by Congress because of such abuses to students' files mentioned in the forgoing cases. FERPA gave much needed protection to student records as well as giving parents access to their children's school records. A non-custodian parent has the same privilege as the custodial parent when viewing the child's educational records. (7)

Administrators and teachers need to understand that FERPA has a stipulation for violating the Act. Federal funds may and can be withdrawn from a school district or any educational institution for the following reasons:

(a) Failing to allow parents have access to their child's educational records.

(b) Sharing information in the records to third parties without the parent's permission. (There are some exceptions to this) [8]

Teachers' daily records of students' progress are confidential as long as they are kept in the possession of the teacher. Teachers should never allow a student to enter grades in the teacher's grade book. Anecdotal notes kept by counselors are privileged as long as the counselor doesn't share those notes with anyone who is not entitled to view the information. Otherwise the counselor can be subpoenaed to court.

Some guidelines to consider before "talking out of shop:"

- Do not make reckless statements with total disregard for the truth.
- Do not make erroneous statements that are known to you be false.
- Do not make statements that cannot be substantiated to be true.

- Statements that may defame a person's reputation.
- Do not make statements or comments that could cause negative consequences for the school system.
- Do not breach confidentiality.
- Do not make statements that are not backed by facts.

Endnotes:

1. *Austin v. Mehville Region 9 School district,* 564 S.W.2d 884 (Mo. 1978)
2. *Lewis v. Harrison School District* No. 1, 621 F.Supp. 1480 (W.D.Ark.1985)
3. *Ferrara v. Mills,* 781 F.2d 1508 (11 Circuit Ct., 1986)
4. *Anderson v. Indiana High School Athletic Association, 699 F.Supp. 719 S.D.Ind. 1988.*
5. *Griswold v. Connecticut,* 381 U.S. 479 (1965).
6. Dawkins v. Billingsley, *172 P. 69 (Oklahoma 1918).*
7. *Page v. Rotterdam-Mohonasen Central School District, 441 N.Y.S,2d 323 (N.Y. Sup.Ct. (1981).*
8. McCarhy, Martha A. and Cambron-McCabe, Nelda H. Public School Law, *Teachers and Students Rights, 3rd Ed. Allyn and Bacon, Boston, Mass. (1992).*

Additional Court Cases

1. *Banks v. Burkich,* 788 F.2d 1161 (6th Cir. 1986).
2. *Ketchens v. Reiner,* 239 Cal.Rptr. 540 (App. 2nd Dist. 1987).
3. *Knapp v. Whittaker,* 757 F.2d 827 (7th Cir. Ct. 1985(
4. *Wichert v. Walter,* 505 F.Supp. 1516 (D.N.J. 1985).
5. *Swilley v. Alexander,* 629 F2d. 1018 (5th Cir. Ct. 1980).
6. *Wren v.Spurlock,* 798 F.2d 1313 (10 Cir. Ct. 1986).

Chapter Nine – EDUCATOR'S LIABILITY

Scores of educators, especially inexperienced teachers, in the public schools are not aware of the liability issues faced in meeting the daily challenges that teachers are confronted on a daily basis.

Working with 18-25 students each hour and helping to maintain a safe and orderly environment in the class, on school trips, during playground activities and other school events, increase the potential for personal liability. This could be as a result of a teacher's action or inaction.

In legal terms, this is the arena of tort law. This type of law deals with any civil wrong and when going to court, the jury will usually award damages. Tort is involved when a person causes damage to a person or a person's property, (real or intangible assets).

The intangible can be toward a person's reputation or character. The teachers' lounge is excellent place for border-line tort to take place as the result of idle or loose gossiping.

Teachers and administrators, like everyone else, are held accountable for their own actions and torts. Governmental immunity does not exempt school employees from tort damages. Teachers have a professional duty to provide "reasonable" care and assistance to injured students commensurate with their training. The "Standard of Care" increases for teachers who are working with severely handicapped special needs children, particularly when they are on trips away from the school. [1]

Courts have acknowledged that schools cannot guarantee the safety of all students (Mawdsley, 2003). [2] Schools officials and school personnel, however, may be legally liable if a student is injured either by a deliberate action or negligence by a teacher.

Usually student injury suits involve tort claims of negligence. Therefore, educators must keep in mind the concepts of preventive law, mentioned previously in the text.

The definition of liability under the United States Constitution is: *"Every person who, under the color of any statute, ordinance, regulation, custom or usage, of any State or "Territory or the District of Columbia, subjects, or causes to be subjected, any citizen of the United States or other person within the jurisdiction thereof to the deprivation of any rights, privileges, or immunities secured by the Constitution and laws, shall be liable to the party injured in action at law, suit in equity, or other proper proceeding for redress…(42 U.S.C., 1983)* [3]

A tort can be classified under the heading of

doing a civil wrong to a person or a person's property and the court awarding damages. This type of activity is decided in a civil court rather than a criminal court of law.

The type of intentional torts that usually involve teachers and administrators come under the headings of (a) assault or battery, (b) false imprisonment, or (c) defamation of character. These along with support cases will be discussed further in this chapter.

Another type of tort is that of *negligence* in the classroom, on school trips, playgrounds and other school sponsored activities. Negligence is an area that can blind-side a person when they get too comfortable on the job and not assuring the degree of care for the safety and well-being of the employees and students. The barometer of measure is that the care or supervision is reasonable and sensible and that any person of sound mind would exercise if presented with that situation.

A high school student was injured while participating in a touch football game which was under the supervision of the physical education teacher. The game became a contact sport out of control in the absence of the teacher who had left the field to go read the daily newspaper. The teacher was not protected under governmental immunity and was found liable for the injury. [4]

If a student gets injured under the supervision of a teacher or administrator, the student must prove the supervision of the adult was not reasonable enough to prevent the injury. The injury of the student must be proven to have been foreseeable before a court will rule on a student's behalf. [5]

Parents filed a suit filed in North Carolina against the School Board on charges of negligence against the shop teacher for not properly supervising the class when their son was injured by a power saw.

The teacher was in an adjoining room teaching while the student was in the shop room working on a project. The teacher replied that each student received adequate instruction on the use of the power saw and the injury was due to the student's negligence. The court agreed with the teacher that the individual instruction of twenty minutes was adequate to prevent an injury on the type of machinery the student was using, even without supervision. [6]

In many situations, tort allegations may be viewed as "errors and omissions." In other words, if one is doing the wrong thing (malfeasance) or perhaps doing the right thing but doing it the wrong way (misfeasance), one is facing extreme scrutiny. Of course if failing to perform a duty which is a contractual responsibility, then the charge is *omission* and

114

the charge of insubordination result in dismissal from the job.

Intentional torts are very common in the schools today, especially with student conflicts. Intentional tort can be in the form of assault, or where one is threatening or attempting to physically harm another person. This type of tort could cause not only physical harm but mental anxiety. A teacher verbally chastising a student could cause some mental discomfort or stress, or even be embarrassing but would not be considered assault.

Battery, another form of assault, has involved many educators who administer corporal punishment. One of the deciding factors whether corporal punishment is identified as an assault or battery, the degree of unreasonableness or cruelty involved. A teacher or administrator should never administer corporal punishment while showing signs of anger. Corporal punishment is and has been interpreted as child abuse. Where is the line drawn between child abuse and corporal punishment? This is the question one should ask before considering the use of corporal punishment. The best advice is "back off" from using corporal punishment as a method to change behavior.

The following case was previously discussed; however, this case further demonstrates tort liability. A third grade female student was paddled by the principal for retaliating toward another student who had kicked the student. This was not a normal method of administering corporal punishment. The principal asks a teacher to hold the student upside down by the ankles while administered the punishment with the paddle. The principal hit the young female student several times on the legs and knees, causing bruises and a severe cut, leaving a permanent scar. Four months later the principal again administered corporal punishment to the young girl. After two blows with the paddle, the student refused another. The principal summoned a male assistant principal to hold the girl over a chair while he again gave three more licks with the paddle. As one would expect with this type of cruel punishment, the child was severely bruised.

The parents of the child sued and the 10th Circuit Court ruled in the parent's favor. The ruling judge made a statement ..." the law was punishment context would violate" a child's right to bodily security. The disturbing wording of the court was that the methods of punishment that are so grossly excessive as to be shocking to the conscience." [7]

If charged with any of the above *torts,* one will be responsible for tortuous behavior. Teachers are not generally covered under government immunity; therefore, it would be wise to get personal liability coverage through an insurance agent. The school board is not responsible for the teacher's defense. Don't look for a "bail out."

Consider the following scenarios:

- A paraprofessional in the classroom is trying to calm an agitated student when suddenly the student throws the books across the room, turns over the desk, and starts hitting the paraprofessional. The teacher takes the student's arms and walks the student into the timeout room. The student struggles, curses, and screams that the teacher is a child abuser and that his parents will sue. The next morning the principal calls and informs the teacher that a policeman is in his office to take a report regarding a possible incident of child abuse. What can you do to protect yourself from this false allegation?

- A fight starting outside the classroom. Two students who are engaged in an argument begin to push and shove each other. The students are instructed to "break it up and report to their next class". One agrees but the other throws a punch at the other student. The student that is grabbed is continuing the confrontation and is led away by the teacher. The student snarls at the teacher, "Get your hands off me, I have my rights." Have the student's rights been violated?

- One of the students attends a general education

classroom for art and music. Because of the aggressive nature of the student, goals have been included on the IEP addressing these frequent outbursts of anger. The IEP team determines that he will be mainstreamed in a few classes; however, the principal believes that, because of confidentiality requirements, the general education teacher should not be told of the student's aggressive tendencies. One day the student attacks and injures a student in art class. Can the teacher be sued for the incident?

- The emotional/behavioral disorders (EBD) class is in the gymnasium for a game of basketball. A student office worker comes in to the gym notifies that the teacher of a phone call in the office. Although there are no adults in the area, the students seem to be involved in their game, so office worker is asked to watch the class while the teacher takes call. While on the phone the student worker runs into the office shouting there has been a fight in the gym. The teacher runs to the gym and finds one of the students lying on the ground, unconscious and bleeding. What is the teacher's liability?

Do any of these scenarios sound familiar? If any of these are familiar, it is not surprising. Incidents like these happen in schools every day. These scenarios were taken from actual events reported in due process hearings or court cases. Would the teacher be required to testify or be cross-examined in a court of law? If so what is the teacher's legal actions? Can the teacher be sued? What is the extent of teacher's liability? Can the teacher or the school be ordered to pay damages? These questions have answers that either appear directly in the law or can be extrapolated from existing laws.

The types of torts which teachers should be knowledgeable of are as follows:

(1) Intentional tort which includes assault or battery. This can sometimes be interpreted in the form of either physical or mental liability. In other words, if a person puts another in a state-of-mind that immediate harm is about to be imposed in an offensive manner, this could be an intentional tort. Assault or battery can also be directed from a student or parent toward a teacher or administrator.

Teachers accused of assault and battery are typically given considerable leeway by the courts (Alexander & Alexander, 1992). [8] This is because assault and battery cases often result from attempts to discipline a student or stop a student from injuring someone. Courts are generally reluctant to interfere with a teacher's authority to discipline students. Courts have found teachers guilty of assault and battery, when a teacher's discipline has been cruel, brutal, excessive, or administered with malice, anger, or intent to injure. [9]

(2) **Negligence** is ignoring one's responsibility in providing the necessary care for keeping a student safe from any harm or danger.

(3) Strict liability is to know there is a risk or danger when students are to handle a tool or chemical while under the teacher's supervision.

(4) **Errors** occur when doing the wrong thing or perhaps performing an experiment, using a tool, etc., the wrong way, resulting in an injury.

(5) **Omission** is failing to do what the assignment requires one to do.

Teachers and administrators using good judgment and common sense can avoid any of the torts listed above.

Endnote:

1. *Mawdsley, R.D., & Russo, C.j. (2003),* FERP*cy and the classroom; What can be learned from Owasso School District v. Salvo? 171 Ed. Law Rep., 397*
2. Lamorte, Michael W. School Law. *Cases and Concepts, 8th ed. Allyn and Bacon, Boston. 1998.*
3. 42 U.S.C., 1983.
4. *Hyman v. Green,* 403 N.W. 2d 597. (Mich. App. (1987).
5. *Roberts v. Robertson County Board of Education.* 692 S.w.2d 863 (Tenn. Ct. App. 1985).
6. *Izard v. Hickory City Schools Board of Education,* 315 S.E.2d 755 (N.C.App.1984) .
7. *Garcia v. Miera,* 817 F.2d 650 (10th Circuit Ct. 1987).
8. *Alexander, K & Alexander M. (2007). American Public School Law, 5th ed. Belmont, Ca: West/Thompson.*
9. *Thompson v. Iberville Parish School Bd. 372 S. 2d.642 (La. Ct.App. 1979), writ denied,* 374 s. 2d 650 (La. 1979).
10. *Baurer v. Minidoka School district.* No. 332, 778 P.2d 336 Div.1990).

Related Court Cases:

1. *Rhea V. Grandview School District, 694 P.2d 666. Wash. Ct. Ap. 1985).*
2. *O'Brien v. Township High School district.* 214, 415 N.E.2ed 1015 (Ill. 1980).
3. *District of Columbia v. Doe,* 524 A.2d 30 (d.c. 1987).
4. *Greene v. City of New York,* 566 N.Y.S.2d 40

(N.Y. ap.Div. 1991).

5. *Poe v. Hamilton,* 565 N.E.2d 887, (Ohio Ct. App. 1990).
6. *Hunter v. Board of Education of Montgomery County*, 292, Maryland. 481, 439 A.2d 585 (1982).
7. *B.M. v. Montana,* 649 P.2d 424 (Montana, 1982)

Chapter Ten – HARASSMENT

Harassment is the type of behavior that goes on in the workplace becomes intolerable and offensive to the targeted person and can quickly create a toxic work environment. Harassment is more common and ignored in the workplace than most people want to believe or admit. Harassment is very seldom a welcomed behavior and can be of a sexual nature which might be severe and pervasive and will affect the employee's performance on the job.

The *Equal Employment Opportunity Commission (EEOC)* which was established in 1964 by *Title VII of the Civil Rights Act* declared sexual harassment to be a violation of *Section 703 of Title VII*. Having made this declaration, the ACT also created a set of guidelines for determining when harassment had sexual overtones of unwelcomed conduct. The ACT is very specific in identifying the criteria for employer liability if this type of offensive conduct by employees is not addressed and corrected. [1]

Sexual Harassment is defined as a form of sex discrimination that involves unwelcomed sexual advances, requests for sexual favors, and other verbal or physical conduct of a sexual nature. This type of harassment can be very obvious or clever, implicit or explicit. It can be quid quo pro, (something for something), such as a promotion or terms of employment. This behavior is unacceptable and illegal and will result in the perpetrator being charged under criminal law.

A female supervisor in a Wisconsin school district complained to district officials that her supervisor was sexually harassing by her propositioning and attempting to kiss her. The complaints were not made in writing but verbally in order to keep the issue at low profile. Because of the complaint, the supervisor was transferred to another office and stripped of the duties. A lawsuit was lodged on the basis that the district retaliated for bringing the issue being to forefront. This was a violation of the First Amendment right to free speech. The court ruled in favor of the school district on grounds that this did not violate the supervisor's right to free speech. [2]

A Missouri vocational teacher lost the assigned job when a male student was allowed to continually sexually harass a female student. The male students were allowed to post centerfolds on the wall without the teacher disciplining the student. The teacher also allowed sexual harassment by bringing a plastic phallus to the classroom. The teacher sued to keep the assigned job, but was denied by the court on the grounds that his behavior constituted immoral conduct. [3]

A teacher in Colorado lost a teaching position because the teacher put his hands on female students. An attempt was made to conceal the teacher's intentions by concealing his intentions by tickling, bodily horseplay and sexual overtones toward the female students. This behavior took place on a field trip in a less structured supervisory capacity. [4] The point to remember is that the teacher has the responsibility to protect the students from any inappropriate behavior and not be the "fox guarding the hen house".

Unwanted sexual advances, requests for sexual favors and other verbal or physical conduct of a sexual nature constitute sexual harassment when:

- "Submission to conduct is made either explicitly or implicitly a term or condition of an individual's employment.

- Submission to or rejection of such conduct by an individual is used as the basis for employment decisions affecting such individual.

- Such conduct has the purpose or effect of unreasonably interfering with an individual's work performance or creating an intimidating, hostile, or offense working environment." C.F.R., Sec. 1604.11 (a) (1991).

- In the case of *Meritor Savings Bank v. Vinson,* the Supreme Court identified two types of sexual harassment. One was involving employment benefits based on sexual favors or "Quid pro Quo". "You do me a favor and I'll return a favor." This could also include promotion, demotion, or termination. The latter two obviously could take place if you don't play the game. [5]

- *Hostile environment*- is another form of sexual harassment. It is a pattern of unwelcome and offensive conduct that unreasonably interferes with an individual's work performance or creates an intimidating or offensive work environment.

The Court warned in the above cases, *"for sexual harassment to be actionable, it must be sufficiently severe or pervasive to alter the conditions of the victim's employment and create an abusive working environment."* [6]

It is paramount that educators understand the implications of the above definitions and how those are intertwined in the work place. Whether a victim of such heinous behavior or initiating such action, it is not acceptable and is punishable by law.

Endnotes:

1. Title VII of the Civil Rights Act, 1980.
2. *Callaway v. Hafeman*, 832 F.2d 414 (7TH Cir. 1987).
3. *Ross v. Robb*, 622 S.W.2d 257 (Mo. 1983)
4. *Weissman v. Board of Education*, 547 P.2d 1267 (Colo. 1976).
5. *Meritor Savings Bank v. Vinson*
6. *Ibid.*

Chapter Eleven – DEVELOPING A DEFENSIVE MINDSET

The previous chapters have identified behavior characteristics causing professional education leaders problems in the workplace, and worse. Many of them had to acquire a defense attorney to protect their integrity, honor, and profession. As one began reflecting on situations that could have been problematic for educators, now is the time to develop a "defensive mindset in order to recognize and avoid the "lurking" dangers that many professionals have ignored.

Identifying Potential Risks

Administrative staff, supervisors and teachers are constantly faced with making choices which have the potential of harming or destroying their career. It is very natural to go with instincts and not consider the consequences of the decision(s) made. Whether the decision of allowing a preschool child to go to the restroom unsupervised, sending a middle school student to the principal's office unsupervised or letting a group of children on a field trip go to multiple fast food places without adequate supervision. There are potential risks involved in all of these scenarios.

Traditionally, because these risks did not materialize where students were injured or worse, the mindset has been to continue

128

following the same "calf path" because it has always been safe. ^{Calf path/wright/Gover/Lowdenback}

When making decisions involving potential risks, several questions should be addressed:

- What is the possibility of harm or damage resulting from this decision?
- Could the harm or damage be serious?
- Will this decision place a career at risk?

As the potential for injury increases, the demand for supervision increases. This is where "risk analysis training" is necessary for public and private school educators because of their responsibility for supervising children. The risk usually increases in vocational classes, special needs classes, physical education class and field trips.

One of the most important defense mechanisms is to have documentation of the rules and regulations posted and made available and explained for understanding. For example, the teacher should have classroom rules posted in a visible place in the room. Having the rules posted may not be enough to protect the teacher, therefore, it is important to have documentation when the rules were read and/or presented to the group when an activity increases the potential risk. A recommendation would be to document the time and date of the rules review in the lesson plan for that particular date. This type of documentation also applies for field trips, playground activities, hallway behavior, and other high risk situations.

Normally, many of the rules are posted in the student discipline code handbook, but that doesn't mean all students or parents read these. The administration should have a schedule set for staff to go over the rules in the student discipline code handbook. The court of law is quite specific in requiring that adequate documentation is available when making a crucial decision involving liability cases.

Several recommendations for an administrator in developing a defensive mindset are listed as follows:

1. Provide and enforce policies and regulations that staff and students must follow. This is crucial and if negated can result in a dangerous and toxic school or organization climate. If employees are allowed to set their own rules or make decisions based upon what they think is best for that particular time and activity, chaos is inevitable.
2. An organization is only as good as the staff employed. Therefore, it is essential that quality and competent personnel are

hired. Certification is not the only criteria for employing the "right" person for the job. The process of hiring must take on a professional approach, i.e., advertising, checking all references and beyond, background checks, and even professional growth records.

3. Provide opportunities for staff development which are appropriate for protecting employees and students. Since many teachers and particularly non-tenured teachers have not been exposed to a course in school law, it is crucial that substantial professional development opportunities in preventive law be made available for the staff.

4. Provide effective supervision and evaluation of staff. This is an area that should not be taken for granted even though it is one of the most essential functions of an administrator. Adequate supervision is part of team building and provides the opportunity to identify those weak links in the team chain that need to be reinforced and corrected.

5. Develop and utilize appropriate and effective communication skills. One may be thinking, "how does this play in establishing a defensive mind set?" The leader must have communication skills in order to share and collaborate with all

stakeholders about the issues the organization has to confront. The leader, to be effective in achieving the goals and objectives of the organization, must establish a "defense" to assure that the employees are astute in avoiding the tragedies of bad decisions. This can only be accomplished if all employees are informed and work collaborative to accomplish the vision and mission of the organization.

6. The leader and staff must be vigilant in knowing their surroundings and recognizing any changes in behavior of staff, students and other stakeholders. This requires being alert, visible and providing constant supervision.

7. Lesson plans should focus on those activities relative to the lesson content. Straying from the content to areas that are controversial and do not relate to the subject matter being taught, has the potential to create controversy.

8. Maintaining adequate documentation of discipline referrals, parent conferences, email communications and telephone calls is essential in establishing a defensive and anticipatory mind set.

9. It is important to be fair and consistent in classroom management and enforcing school rules. Many know that this is an

area that creates conflict for teachers, students and parents. Teachers and administrators must include appropriate stakeholders in this process. This is part of the collaborative and supervision model that the administrator must follow.

10. Be prepared to modify behavior and/or the decision making process. If one is fortunate enough to avoid the wrath of the court or school board after making a poor judgment call, then that experience must be used to modify behavior and create an anticipatory mind set.

A CONSIDERATION OF POLICIES AFFECTED BY LEGAL CHALLENGES

Be prepared to change one's actions, behavior and/or decision-making process! *It has been stated, "The best offense is a good defense." This requires discipline, study, implementation, knowledge, discipline, etc. A good offense just doesn't happen without these ingredients. The many cases described in the book happened because of not being informed of policies and laws, being incompetent, or stupid. So where does one go from here?*

The following pages hopefully will suggest some ideas and guidelines to keep educators out of mediation, litigation, and the court of law.

Chapter Twelve – LEGAL IMPLICATIONS OF THE ROLE OF THE PRINCIPAL

Staff Relations and Collaboration

Traditionally, many school leaders have failed to use the process of *Collaboration* effectively. Collaboration is a communications process that brings all the key players together to focus on the issue or challenge at hand.

It has been proven that school reform isn't possible without involving all the key players in the school. This includes the teaching staff, department heads and others as needed. A coach doesn't depend upon one player to have a winning season and in every case it is "teamwork" that fosters success. There is no "I" in team!

The general does not win a war without having troops on the ground. The teaching staff and department heads are the troops on the ground. They are the eyes and ears of what is going on in the school and what changes need to be made to improve the learning and achievement of students.

The legal aspect of frequent classroom visits as outlined in the *Kentucky Principal Professional Growth and Effectiveness System (PPGES)* where the principal is required to evaluate the effectiveness of the teachers is paramount. This allows the principal to identify potential issues which could affect the safety of the students and /or the career of the teacher, if not caught early. If the leader delays taking necessary steps until a classroom crisis happens, not only will the teacher's future be in jeopardy, but the administrator as well.

Principals must be highly visible in and out of the classroom and other parts of the building. An effective leader will maintain a schedule which allows visibility throughout the educational facility. This routine will improve the principal's professional leadership stature. It will give the staff more confidence in the leader. To put it plainly, the message is "do as I do, not as I say". The more visible the principal, the more confidence faculty and staff will have with the leadership.

Effective Policies in Place

The school principal is responsible for insuring that policies are in place to operate a smooth, safe and effective school. It is necessary that the principal understand what the school board policies require as well as state and federal laws and regulations.

Being in violation of any of those laws, policies and regulations could result in the loss of not only the position of principal, but could mean the revocation of the principal's teaching and administrative licenses.

135

So, when accepting a principal's position, it is implicit that the principal understands the ramifications of any and all decisions affected by school board policy, state and federal laws and regulations. Adherence to all laws, policies and regulations, are an ultra-high priority. Ignorance is not sufficient for making "bad" or ineffective decisions, especially when there is a plethora of information outlined in board policy, state and federal laws and administrative regulations. (Wright and Gover)

Special Education

This is an area that is easy to administer provided the school administrator maintains an open mind and has a desire to solve the problem and has a clear understanding of the laws governing special education. The Principal and special education personnel must know the laws and be mindful of how to apply those laws to insure what is best for the child is in place.

Parents will work with the principal if given half a chance. In many instances parents feel shunned and intimidated by the school. (Wright and Gover)

How Would You as
A School Administrator
Handle This Challenge?

Here is an example where the principal and a two teachers and a parent came to an impasse.

In a county school district, a new superintendent's first order of business, was to deal with a child where the mother requested for the child to be placed in a regular classroom and receive special education services in the regular classroom. The federal law states students should be placed in the "least restrictive" environment.

This issue had festered to the point based upon the lack of leadership of the principal where it was necessary to convene an Administrative Admissions and Release Committee (AARC).

The speech and language pathologist said that "this would be appropriate for the child and she could take care of the student's speech/language issues in the regular classroom" and in many cases help other students in the process.

There were several professional educators and one lone parent at the table. The parent looked as though the world was on the mother's shoulders. The parent was poorly dressed and stated that it was felt that the decision would not be fair for her child.

Since the superintendent would be chairing this very important committee, the superintendent looked at the board policy, state and federal laws and administrative regulations and also conducted interviews with the special education teachers and other regular teachers.

The superintendent asked the Special Education Director to coordinate the meeting. Since the parent did not have anyone advocating for the family and child, the superintendent moved to the space next to where the mother was sitting as said "that he would be the advocate for the child". After a few minutes of discussion, the AARC committee voted to put the child in a regular classroom receiving special education services in addition to the curriculum that was taught in the regular classroom. This placement worked out spectacularly with the child meeting much success in that placement. (Wright and Gover)

It appears in this case that the principal did not provide the leadership necessary to deal with complicated issues such as this. A leader would have solved the problem at the classroom and school level. When the principal shows ineffective leadership, the problem is just to "kick the can" down the road and let someone else solve the problem. Answer the following questions.

1. Was the superintendent dealing with this situation appropriately?
2. Should the principal have solved the problem at the school level?
3. How could this issue have been solved?

4. How did this issue evolve to the level of an AARC?

Guidance and Counseling

This is an area where many school principals miss the boat entirely. The school principal must recognize that young people today live in a complex world. They are exposed at a much earlier age to pressures of the adult life and do not have the experience or family supports as students in the past. School for many students is the main source of stability and guidance in their lives. The guidance counselors play a fundamental role in ensuring that every aspect of the school comes into play in helping children and youth make necessary adjustments to the challenges in school as well as life challenges. (Wright and Gover)

Department Job Descriptions

At no time should the school guidance and counseling program be placed in a situation that meets out punishment or discipline. The counselor must always be in a neutral position with the students, so that trust and open communication is always available for the student.

Various departmental job descriptions are supplied herein for new administrators, who may not be familiar with the legal ramifications and liabilities of the decisions made by the staff in the different departments.

These departments are staffed with personnel who are "trained" and "certified" specifically to make decisions which are in the best interest for the students. Therefore, it is imperative that building principals do not micromanage these departments. An example: The assistant principal **tells** the guidance secretary to **tell** the counselor to cover the **behavior modification room** for an hour". Two things are inappropriate in this scenario:

(1) The chain of command: The assistant principal should have gone directly to the counselor with the request, which would have given the counselor an opportunity to clarify the role of counselors.
(2) The request was inappropriate and would have placed the counselor in a position of being a disciplinarian. The assistant principal should have covered the behavior modification room.

School Nurse

The National Association of School Nurses states "that the registered professional school nurse is the leader in the school community to oversee school health policies and programs". The school nurse serves in a pivotal role to provide expertise and oversight for the provision of school health services and promotion of health education. Using clinical knowledge and judgment, the school nurse provides health care to students and staff, performs health screenings and coordinates referrals to the medical home or private healthcare provider. The school nurse serves as a liaison between school personnel, family, community and healthcare providers to advocate for health care and a healthy school environment (American Nurses Association & National Association of School Nurses [ANA & NASN], 2011).

Staffing/Personnel

The principal is responsible for overseeing all faculty/staff in the building. The principal is accountable for interviewing prospective candidates for job openings within their building as well as making recommendations to the superintendent for hiring new teachers as well as noncertified staff. It is the principal's obligation, after collaborating with the appropriate faculty and staff, to insure that the most effective candidate is recommended for any vacant position. (Wright and Gover)

Budgeting and Finance

The principal ensures that the school bookkeeper or secretary maintains appropriate records in accordance with the Laws and Regulation developed by the state. This involves the bookkeeping records, bank reconciliation statements, petty cash records, receipts and any other record that would apply to accounting of funds from their inception to expenditure. It is the principals' responsibility to ensure that proper procedures for withdrawals are followed and obtaining the signatures necessary to fulfill the obligation of state laws and board policies. (Wright and Gover)

Principals must continually monitor the spending, seeing to it that the funds are spent in a timely manner and that receipts and copies of bills accompany each payment. The principal ensures that financial reports are made as required by law. Principals insure that the bookkeeper or school secretary has financial records and reports for the Board and also advise the Board on expenditures from school accounts. It is the principals' responsibility to ensure that: (1) disbursements are recorded properly, (2) a record is kept of all materials purchased from public funds, and (3) and the books are audited annually according to board policies. In Kentucky, Principals will follow the guidelines outlined in the <u>Accounting Procedures for Kentucky School Activity Funds, July 1, 2013.</u>

Endnotes:

1. *American Nurses Association & National Association of School Nurses [ANA & NASN], 2011.*

2. *Accounting Procedures for Kentucky School Activity Funds, July 1, 2013.*

Chapter Thirteen – CHURCH AND STATE IN PUBLIC EDUCATION

This is an issue that public school leaders have been wrestling with since the beginning of public funding of education. Thomas Jefferson and the founding fathers wanted to make sure that America maintained a separation of church and state. American was founded upon the basis of "freedom of religion". Thomas Jefferson said, *"I consider the government of the United States as interdicted by the Constitution from intermeddling with religious institutions, their doctrines, discipline, or exercises.* [1]

More than likely this will be a never ending challenge for public school officials. It is incumbent upon public school leaders, teachers, principals, superintendents and boards of education, to know and understand the law and to be very much aware of pitfalls that *can* and will befall them if the law is not followed. In the next few pages' an important aspect of church/state which affect public schools will be addressed. This could be a guide to keeping school leaders out of litigation.

Definition of Church and State

It is a fact that school districts must be neutral toward religion. Separation of church and state is fundamental as required by the First Amendment. It allows all citizens the freedom to practice any religion of their choice; however, it also prevents public schools, *which is the government*, from officially favoring any religion.

"A phrase most famously used by Supreme Court Justice Black in the case of Everson v. Board of Education. In discussing the Establishment Clause of the First Amendment, Justice Black said that the clause erected a *"wall of separation between church and state."* He explained that this means, among other things, that the government cannot participate in the affairs of a religious group, set up a church, aid or prefer one religion over another, or aid or prefer religion over non-religion." [2]

Separation of Church and State
"A landmark decision Agostini v. Felton is a significant decision of the Supreme Court of the United states. In this case, the Court overruled its decision made in 1987 finding that it was not a violation of the Establishment Clause of the first Amendment for a state-sponsored education initiative to allow public school teachers to instruct at religious schools, so long as the material was secular and neutral in nature and no "excessive entanglement" between government and religion was apparent. This case is noteworthy in a broader sense as a sign of evolving judicial standards surrounding the First Amendment, and the changes that have occurred in modern Establishment Clause Jurisprudence." [3]

Here are a couple of quotes that "strike to the heart" of Church and State relations.

- *"When the government puts its imprimatur on a particular religion it conveys a message of exclusion to all those who do not adhere to the favored beliefs. A government cannot be premised on the belief that all persons are created equal when it asserts that God prefers some." Supreme Court Justice Harry A. Blackmun.* [4]

- *"You don't believe in Separation of Church and State? Well, since you want your church to tell the government how to govern, does that mean the government can come into your church and tell you how to worship? Separation is for the protection of both." Zoe Anadon* [5]

Student Led Prayers

"The principle that government may accommodate the free exercise of religion does not supersede the fundamental limitations imposed by the Establishment Clause. It is beyond dispute that, at a minimum, the Constitution guarantees that government may not coerce anyone to support or participate in religion or its exercise, or otherwise act in a way which `establishes a [state] religion or religious faith, or tends to do so." Lynch v. Don-elly, 465 U. S. 678 (1984). [6]

"This is one of the most confusing and controversial areas of the current school prayer debate. While the courts have not clarified all of the issues, some are clearer than others. For instance, inviting outside adults to lead prayers at graduation ceremonies is clearly unconstitutional. The Supreme Court resolved this issue in the 1992 case Lee v. Weisman, which began when prayers were delivered by clergy at a middle school's commencement exercises in Providence, Rhode Island."

The school designed the program, provided for the invocation, selected the clergy, and even supplied guidelines for the prayer. Therefore, the Supreme Court held that the practice violated the First Amendment's prohibition against laws "respecting an establishment of religion." The majority based its decision on the fact that (1) it is not the business of schools to sponsor or organize religious activities, and (2) students who might have objected to the prayer were subtly coerced to participate. This psychological coercion was not resolved by the fact that attendance at the graduation was "voluntary." In the Court's view, few students would want to miss the culminating event of their academic career.

A murkier issue is student-initiated, student-led prayer at school-sponsored events. On one side of the debate are those who believe that student religious speech at graduation ceremonies or other school-sponsored events violates the Establishment Clause. They are bolstered by the 2000 Supreme Court case of Santa Fe v. Doe,[2] which involved the traditional practice of student-led prayers over the public address system before high school football games. According to the district, students would vote each year on whether they would have prayers at home football games. If they decided to do so, they would then select a student to deliver the prayers. To ensure fairness, the school district said it required these prayers to be "non-sectarian [and] non-proselytizing."

A 6 to 3 majority of the Supreme Court still found the Santa Fe policy to be unconstitutional. The majority opinion first pointed out that constitutional rights are not subject to a vote.

To the contrary, the judges said the purpose of the Bill of Rights was to place some rights beyond the reach of political majorities. Thus, the Constitution protects a person's right to freedom of speech, press, or religion even if no one else agrees with the ideas a person professes.[3]

In addition, the Court found that having a student, as opposed to an adult, lead the prayer did not solve the constitutional dilemma. A football game is still a school-sponsored event, they held, and the school was still coercing the students, however subtly, to participate in a religious exercise.

Finally, the Court ruled that the requirement that the prayer be "non-sectarian" and "non-proselytizing" not only failed to solve the problems addressed in Lee v. Weisman, it may have aggravated them.[5] In other words, while some might like the idea of an inclusive, nonsectarian "civil" religion, others might not. To some people, the idea of nonsectarian prayer is offensive, as though a prayer were being addressed "to whom it may concern." Moreover, the Supreme Court made clear in Lee v. Weisman that even nondenominational prayers or generic religiosity may not be established by the government at graduation exercises.

Another thorny part of this issue is determining whether a particular prayer tends to proselytize. Such determinations entangle school officials in religious matters in unconstitutional ways. In fact, one Texas school district was sued for discriminating against those who wished to offer more sectarian prayers at graduation exercises.

On the other side of this debate are those who contend that not allowing students to express themselves religiously at school events violates the students' free exercise of religion and free speech rights. Case law indicates, however, that this may be true only in instances involving strictly student speech, and not when a student is conveying a message controlled or endorsed by the school. As the 11th Circuit case of Adler v. Duval County suggests, it would seem possible for a school to provide a forum for student speech within a graduation ceremony when prayer or religious speech might occur.

For example, a school might allow the valedictorian or class president an opportunity to speak during the ceremony. If such a student chose to express a religious viewpoint, it seems unlikely it would be found unconstitutional unless the school had suggested or otherwise encouraged the religious speech. In effect, this means that in order to distance itself from the student's remarks, the school must create a limited open forum for student speech in the graduation program.

Again, there is a risk for school officials in this approach. By creating a limited open forum for student speech, the school may have to accept almost anything the student wishes to say. Although the school would not be required to allow speech that was profane, sexually explicit, defamatory, or disruptive, the speech could include political or religious views offensive to many, as well as speech critical of school officials.

If school officials feel a solemnizing event needs to occur at a graduation exercise, a neutral moment of silence might be the best option. This way, everyone could pray, meditate, or silently reflect on the previous year's efforts in her own way." [7]

Vaccination Case in New York Public Schools

Children whose parents opt them out of vaccines on religious grounds can be barred from New York City's public schools if the child poses a threat to another pupil, a federal judge has ruled. U. S. District Judge William F. Kuntz II found that education officials can send unvaccinated children home when another student suffers from a vaccinated preventable disease. [8]

Note: The above Court references need to be part of your repertoire and knowledge

base as teachers and administrators, to assure success and longevity in the educational arena.

Endnotes

1. Letter of Thomas Jefferson to the Danbury Baptist Association, Connecticut, January 1, 1802.
2. Definition from Nolo's Plain-English Law Dictionary.
3. U.S. Supreme Court ruling, Agostini v. Felton (1997), at: http://caselaw.lp.findlaw.com/
4. Supreme Court Justice Harry A. Blackmun Quote on Separation of Church and State.
5. *Zoe Anadon – Separation of Church and State Issues Quote.*
6. Lynch v. Don-nelly, 465 U. S. 688, 687 (1984).
7. www.firstamendments.schools.ort/freedoms/faq .aspx?12811 & printer-friendly=y
8. U. S. District Judge William F. Kuntz II found that education officials can send unvaccinated children home when another student suffers from a vaccine preventable disease. Article written on June 25, 2014, by Sarah Jones of Wall of Separation Journal.

Additional Case References *Lee v. Weisman*, 505 U.S. 577 (1992).

- *Santa Fe Independent Sch. Dist. v. Doe*, 530 U.S. 290 (2000).

- *Adler v. Duval County*, 250 F.3d 1330 (11th Cir. 2001), cert. denied, 122 S. Ct. 664 (2001).

- See *Doe v. Madison Sch. Dist.*, 177 F.3d 789 (9th Cir. 1998, vacated on other grounds); *Adler v. Duval County*, 250 F.3d 1330 (11th Cir. 2001), cert. denied, 122 S. Ct. 664 (2001).

APPENDIX

Steps for Teacher and Administrator Certification taken from EPSB Website

Candidates Trained in Kentucky will need the following:

- A completed CA-1 application form (.pdf)

- **OFFICIAL** transcripts of all graduate and undergraduate coursework

- Verification by the Superintendent or Personnel Director of full-time classroom teaching experience at the appropriate grade level(s) (Section 2 of CA-1)

- Passing Praxis II Specialty Area test scores for EACH area of certification and the Principles of Learning and Teaching test score for appropriate grade range

- A completed state **and** federal background check (with full name, date of birth, and last four digits of SSN)

- Verification of completion of teacher preparation program from the preparing college or university (Section 5 of CA-1)

- A $50 money order or certified check made payable to the "Kentucky State Treasurer" or applicants may also use EPSB "E-Pay" online payment service to pay certification fees once the completed application has been mailed.

Candidates Trained out of State will need the following:

- A completed a CA-1 application. Forward this application to your college for the completion of

155

Section IV on page 5 of the CA-1 application.

- Passing <u>Praxis II</u> Specialty Area test scores for EACH area of certification (if less than two years of appropriate full-time teaching experience) and the Principles of Learning and Teaching test score for appropriate grade range.

- A completed state **and** federal background check (with full name, date of birth, and last four digits of SSN)

- Completion of CA-1 Section II by your superintendent, if you have out-of-state teaching experience.

- A $50 money order or certified check made payable to the "Kentucky State Treasurer" or applicants may also use EPSB <u>"E-Pay"</u> online payment service to pay certification fees once the completed application has been mailed.

- **OFFICIAL** transcripts of all college and graduate coursework sent to:

Additional Information:

Out-of-state applicants must have completed a state approved teacher preparation program at a regionally accredited educator preparation institution or a state-approved alternative training program. In addition, candidates must comply with the state ancillary requirements such as GPA, testing and internship.

Out-of-state applicants who hold a valid certificate and have completed two (2) years of teaching in the subject area and grade level on their certificate will be waived of the current testing requirements.

Candidates Trained outside the U.S. will need the following:

- A four-year bachelor's degree teacher preparation program which includes a sequence of professional education courses
- Practice teaching or student teaching component
- A cumulative 2.5 grade point average or 3.0 on the last 60 hours of coursework
- Copy of foreign teaching credential
- A teaching area recognized by Kentucky as an area of certification
- A completed state **and** federal background check (with full name, date of birth, and last four digits of SSN)

Additional Information:

Applicants with foreign training must meet the same academic requirements as applicants trained in the United States and submit the documentation listed above. A course-by-course evaluation MUST also be submitted from one of the approved evaluation agencies indicating that the foreign degree(s) meet(s) the above criteria. In addition to the approved agencies seen via the links above and below, the EPSB also recognizes course-by-course evaluations conducted by the American Association of Collegiate Registrars and Admissions Officers. (http://www.aacrao.org/)

Statement of Eligibility (SOE) Renewal (Teacher)

- The SOE allows candidates five (5) years to apply and receive employment as a teacher in a Kentucky school. During the first year of employment, the Kentucky Teacher Internship Program (KTIP) must be successfully completed.

- If the internship is not completed within the five (5) year period, the applicant may renew the SOE by repeating and passing the assessment program in effect for new teachers at that time or by completing a minimum of six (6) graduate hours toward completion of a graduate program required by administrative regulations promulgated by the Education Professional Standards Board.

- The option for renewal through completion of graduate hours shall be available only for the first renewal.

Certification for Administrators

Contact the Kentucky EPSB Website to learn the procedures for the completion of certifications each of the areas listed:

- Certification for School Principal
- Certification for Guidance Counseling
- Certification for School Superintendent
- Certification for Supervisor of Instruction
- Certification for Director of Special Education
- Certification for Directors of Pupil Personnel

National Board Certification and Acceptance to a Principal Certification Program

A teacher aspiring to become a school principal/administrator should check with their State's Certification Department before starting the process, especially if they have attained Rank I or Rank II, in Kentucky, through the National Board Certification process. Kentucky is one of the states that requires a Master's degree to be admitted to the Principal Program. Further, it is advised that before starting their graduate course work toward becoming a certified school administrator in any state, they should check to see what steps are required by the State Department of Education in that state. Getting National Board Certified as a teacher in some states may not preclude earning a master's degree for the purpose of being admitted to a Principal Certification program. (Kentucky Educational Professional Board)

Division of Certification
Education Professional Standards Board
100 Airport Road, 3rd Floor
Frankfort, Kentucky 40601

JOB DESCRIPTIONS

Title: Guidance Counselor – Elementary, Middle and High Levels

Qualifications:
1. At least three years of successful teaching experience.
2. An endorsement as a Guidance Counselor.
3. A Master's Degree, or its equivalent, representing intensive course work in the principles and practice of educational guidance; educational testing and measurement; counseling; and organization and administration of guidance services; and the psychology of learning.
4. Such other qualifications as the Board may find appropriate.

Terms of Employment:
The Guidance Counselor shall, under normal circumstances, be elected by the Board no later than April 15. Contract terms shall be established by the Board Salary and Fringe Benefits as adopted by the Board for certified staff.

Reports to:
School Principals

Job Goals
To help elementary, middle and high school students to overcome problems that impede learning and social growth, and to personally and directly assist in preparing them to make life decisions.

Essential Job Functions

1. Coordinate the orientation of students to the elementary, middle and high school levels.
2. Work with students on an individual or small group basis in the solution of personal problems as related to peers, home and family, health, and emotional adjustment.
3. Be available to students so as to provide counseling that will lead to increased personal growth, self-understanding, and maturity.
4. Under the auspices of the principal, select and administer, and/or coordinate the standardized testing efforts of the attendance area schools.
5. Assist the principal in maintaining the permanent cumulative file for each student and assure appropriateness and currency.
6. Assist students, staff and parents in evaluating student aptitudes and abilities through the interpretation of individual standardized test scores and other pertinent data, and work with them in developing the students' educational plans.
7. Work with other staff to integrate career exploration into the regular curriculum.
8. Monitor the progress of elementary, middle and high school graduates for the purpose of improving not only the guidance and counseling services, but also evaluating the effectiveness of the school educational programs.
9. Be a member of the Child Study Team in the development of an IEP for handicapped students.

10. Maintain communications with administration, faculty, and parents so as to better meet the needs of each student.
11. Be actively involved in and serve as a resource person for the teacher/student advisor program of the school.
12. Recognize the extent of his/her training and refer to other specialists those pupils whose problems go beyond his/her skills.
13. Implement, direct, and coordinate the in-class guidance program for elementary and middle level students.

Other Job Functions:

Perform such other tasks and assume such other responsibilities as may be assigned by the Principal, provided such assignments do not diminish the effectiveness of the counselor.

Evaluation:

Performance of this job will be evaluated by the principal in agreement with the provisions of the Board's policy on evaluation of certified personnel.

SCHOOL NURSE

School Nurse General Responsibilities:
Manage and coordinate the assigned school's health services program in a school or district based on requirements established by the state and local board policies, procedures, and protocols.

Essential Job Function:
1. Ensure compliance with procedures, protocols, and other instructions provided by the coordinator of health services or contained in division manuals and protocols.
2. Provide nursing care and physical screening to students; assess students and implement first aid measures for students as needed.
3. Assume responsibility for appropriate assessment, planning, intervention, evaluation, management, and referral activities for students.
4. Counsel with students concerning problems such as pregnancy, sexually transmitted diseases and substance abuse in order to facilitate responsible decision making practices.
5. Implement and record required screening programs; notify parents when further medical evaluation is indicated.
6. Establish and update health and immunization records. • Prepare and maintain student clinic records and prepare required reports.
7. Administer daily and PRN (as needed) medications and nursing care procedures prescribed by the student's physician.
8. Initiate emergency procedures for students and staff as needed.

9. Develop Individual Health Care Plans and 504 Plans for students on a case by case basis.
10. Complete the preliminary nursing assessments and assist the physician with the child study physical examinations for students in the child study process.
11. Orient the staff and teach specific medical procedures for the evaluation and maintenance of the medically involved student in the classroom.
12. Present, train and maintain appropriate standards from OSHA regarding contact with, and possible exposure to blood borne pathogens and other potentially infectious body materials within the school or employment setting.
13. Provide health education and anticipatory counseling.
14. Follow procedures for suspected cases of child abuse and neglect.
15. Act as a liaison between the school, home health department professionals, and other community agencies.

Education and Experience:

Graduate from an accredited nursing program; Bachelor of Nursing Degree preferred and licensed as a registered nurse, and in good standing with the State License Requirements. Possess a Valid CPR certification Possession of a valid driver's license

PRINCIPAL

Contract Length: 12 Month

Reports to: Superintendent and will complete any and all assignments as required by the Superintendent.

Instructional Leadership:
1. Assumes responsibility and instructional leadership for the planning, operation, supervision, and evaluation of the educational program.
2. Communicates with students, teachers, parents and community members using a variety of mediums including technology.
3. Partners with teachers to evaluate the effectiveness of instruction and individual teacher performance.
4. Coordinates and promotes professional growth plans and opportunities for faculty and staff.
5. Coordinates New Teacher Induction and ongoing staff development program
6. Establishes a professional development plan for all building level administrators with on-going dialogue, reflection, and evaluation.
7. Provides leadership and oversight for the instructional, co-curricular and extra-curricular programs.
8. Responsible for horizontal and vertical articulation and curricular alignment.

9. Works with teachers and parents to implement student interventions that differentiate instruction based on student need.
10. Reviews curriculum development proposals.
11. Oversees assessment program.
12. Establishes, monitors, and evaluates school improvement goals as documented in the annual School Improvement Plan.
13. Uses data to make decisions about curriculum, assessment, instruction and all school improvement efforts.
14. Establishes a culture of mutual respect and excellence through dialogue and relationships with staff, students, central office administrators, and community members.
15. Develops, monitors, and evaluates programs to enhance positive school culture and climate.
16. Responsible for staffing, enrollment, and budget decisions involving master schedule development.
17. Coordinates selection of all certified and classified staff.

Management:
1. Develops Building Master Schedule and Staff Supervision Schedule.
2. Develops and monitors overall school and departmental budgets.
3. Ultimately responsible for building operations and maintenance.
4. Interprets Board of Education and central office policies and procedures.

5. Maintains student handbook and building procedures.
6. Responsible for student management, attendance and discipline.
7. Oversees the inventory, purchase, and organization of textbooks and supplies.
8. Oversees vendor and service contracts.
9. Coordinates building level crisis plan.
10. Supervises school activities and events.

Education and Experience:
1. Graduate from an accredited program.
2. Hold a Master's Degree and in good standing with the State License Requirements.
3. Minimum of three years' experience as a supervising principal.

SPECIAL EDUCATION TEACHER

Essential Job Functions:

The special education teacher accepts the responsibility of educating children in grades preschool through twelfth grade who are diagnosed with a number of physical, mental and emotional disabilities.

- The teacher leads the collecting of the legally required paperwork.
- The special education teacher insures that each child has an IEP, or Individualized Educational Plan, that outlines the necessary supports, accommodations and goals for each identified student.
- Through the IEP each student can meet both academic and behavioral concerns.
- The special education teacher leads meetings with parents and staff regarding the plan and makes necessary adjustments throughout the year.
- The special education teacher work with children who can vary from mild to severe disabilities, using specialized techniques to help them reach their education goals.

Responsibilities:

The Special education teacher will collaborate with staff to assist in the identification children who qualify for the program. This may include regular education, art, music and physical educational teachers, support staff, physical and occupational therapists and administration.

Recordkeeping and Disposition:

The special education teacher is responsible for record keeping for all identified children from the beginning of the identification process until the students exits the program.

- The special education teacher must have the personality to deal with problem behaviors and serving as a source of information and support in the regular classroom.
- The special education teacher may work as co-teachers in a regular classroom with a general education teacher as well in many instances the speech and language pathologists.
- The special education teacher must have a positive propensity for collaborating with others and understand the importance of teamwork in working with parents, administration and other teachers.

The special education teacher must maintain a professional attitude and the ability to work under pressure.

Training and Certification Requirements:

- B.A. in Special Education
- Master of Arts in Special Education
- Certification by State Accrediting Agency

Assignment:

The Special Education Teacher is answerable to the immediate supervisor which is usually the principal of the school where assigned.

INDEX

A

appropriate conduct, 1
Average Daily Attendance, 58

B

Bullying and Harassment, 62

C

Cales v. Howell Public Schools, 101
Child Abuse Law, 52
Child Abuse Law in Kentucky, 52
code of ethics, 70, 81
comfort zone, 25
concept of reasonableness, 100
Conduct and Association, 95
Copyright Issues, 64
Corporal Punishment, 45
crossed the line, 5, 84

D

Definition of Church and State, 144
Different Life Style, 92

E

EDUCATOR'S LIABILITY, 111
educators, 1, 2, 3, 4, 16, 28, 37, 53, 64, 76, 77, 78, 81, 82, 83, 84, 86, 87, 92, 93, 111, 112, 115, 126, 129, 137
educators' conduct, 2
Equal Employment Opportunity Commission, 123
example set by the teacher, 85

F

Family Educational Rights and Privacy Act, 107
Fifth Amendment, 16, 20, 45, 66
First Amendment, 15, 18, 20, 69, 70, 72, 73, 75, 76, 78, 90, 92, 106, 124
Fourteenth Amendment, 16, 73
Fourth Amendment, 16, 100, 102
freedom of speech, 16, 18, 69, 74, 75, 106

G

Gilbertson v. McAlister,, 76, 79
Givhan v. Western Line Consolidated School District, 74, 79
good faith, 51
Griswold v. Connecticut, 107, 110
Guidance and Counseling, 139

H

HARASSMENT, 123
Hopkins County Board of Education, 88
Horosko v. School District of Mr. Pleasant in 1939, 85

I

Incompetency, 30
ineffective teaching, 32
Instructional Time, 61
Insubordination, 33

170

171

Student Rights, 45, 67
Students' records, 107

T

talking out of shop, 108
teacher's gestures, 86
teachers' lounge, 105, 111
tort law, 111

U

Unauthorized Sick Leave, 37

unfitness, 83, 94
unreasonable actions, 49
Using Reasonable Judgment, 53

V

**Vaccination Case in New
    York Public Schools**, 152

W

wrongful act, 2

www.ingramcontent.com/pod-product-compliance
Lightning Source LLC
La Vergne TN
LVHW051633080426
835511LV00016B/2326